W9-BMP-128

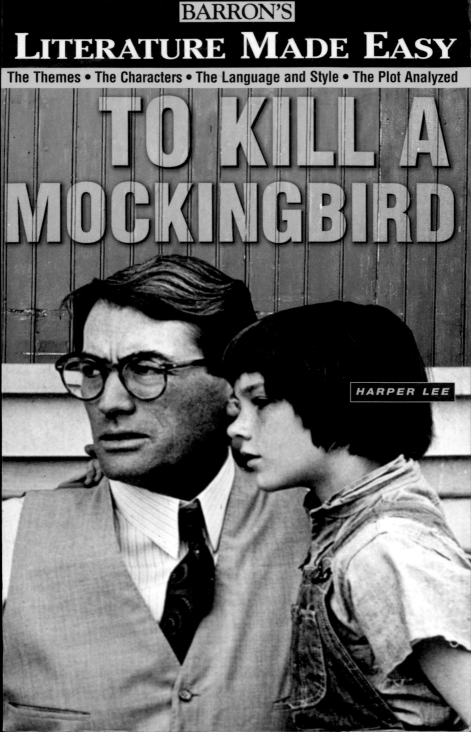

LITERATURE MADE EASY

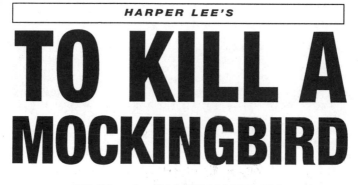

HARPER LEE'S

TO KILL A MOCKINGBIRD

Written by MARY HARTLEY
WITH TONY BUZAN

BARRON'S

First edition for the United States and Canada published by Barron's Educational Series, Inc., 1999.

Copyright © 1999 U.S. version, Barron's Educational Series, Inc.

First published in the United Kingdom by Hodder & Stoughton Ltd. Under the title:
A Guide to To Kill a Mockingbird

Copyright © 1988 Mary Hartley
Introduction Copyright © 1998 Tony Buzan

Cover photograph © The Ronald Grant Archive
Mind Maps: Ann Jones
Illustrations: Karen Donnelly

Mary Hartley asserts the moral right to be identified as the author of this work.

American text edited by Benjamin Griffith.

All inquiries should be addressed to:
Barron's Educational Series, Inc.
250 Wireless Boulevard
Hauppauge, New York 11788
http://www.barronseduc.com

ISBN-13: 978-0-7641-0822-8
ISBN-10: 0-7641-0822-0

Library of Congress Catalog Card No. 98-73081

PRINTED IN THE UNITED STATES OF AMERICA
19 18 17

ONTENTS

There are five important things you must know about your brain and memory to revolutionize
the way you study:

◆ how your memory
("recall") works *while* you are learning
◆ how your memory works *after* you have finished learning
◆ how to use Mind Maps – a special technique for helping you with all aspects of your studies
◆ how to prepare for tests and exams.

Recall during learning
— THE NEED FOR BREAKS

When you are studying, your memory can concentrate, understand, and remember well for between 20 and 45 minutes at a time, then it needs a break. If you continue for longer than this without a break, your memory starts to break down. If you study for hours nonstop, you will remember only a small fraction of what you have been trying to learn, and you will have wasted hours of valuable time.

So, ideally, *study for less than an hour*, then take a five- to ten-minute break. During the break listen to music, go for a walk, do some exercise, or just daydream. (Daydreaming is a necessary brain-power booster – geniuses do it regularly.) During the break your brain will be sorting out what it has been learning, and you will go back to your books with the new information safely stored and organized in your memory. We recommend breaks at regular intervals as you work through this book. Make sure you take them!

Recall *after learning*

– THE WAVES OF YOUR MEMORY

What do you think begins to happen to your
memory right after you have finished learning something?
Does it immediately start forgetting? No! Your brain actually
increases its power and continues remembering. For a short
time after your study session, your brain integrates the
information, making a more complete picture of everything it
has just learned. Only then does the rapid decline in memory
begin, and as much as 80 percent of what you have learned can
be forgotten in a day.

However, if you catch the top of the wave of your memory,
and briefly review (look back over) what you have been
studying at the correct time (while your brain is continuing to
remember), the memory is imprinted far more strongly, and
stays at the crest of the wave for a much longer time. To
maximize your brain's power to remember, take a few minutes
at the end of a day and use a Mind Map to review what you
have learned. Then review it at the end of a week, again at the
end of a month, and finally a week before your test or exam.
That way you'll ride your memory
wave all the way there – and beyond!

The Mind Map ®

– A PICTURE OF THE WAY YOU THINK

Do you like taking notes? More important, do you like having to
go back over and learn them before tests or exams? Most
students I know certainly do not! And how do you take your
notes? Most people take notes on lined paper, using blue or
black ink. The result, visually, is boring. And what does *your*
brain do when it is bored? It turns off, tunes out, and goes to
sleep! Add a dash of color, rhythm, imagination, and the whole
note-taking process becomes much more fun, uses more of your
brain's abilities, and improves your recall and understanding.

Generally, your Mind Map is highly personal and need not be
understandable to any other person. It mirrors *your* brain. Its
purpose is to build up your "memory muscle" by creating
images that will help you recall instantly the most important

points about the characters and plot sequences in a work of fiction you are studying.

You will find Mind Maps throughout this book. Study them, add some color, personalize them, and then try drawing your own – you'll remember them far better. Stick them in your files and on your walls for a quick-and-easy review of the topic.

HOW TO DRAW A MIND MAP

1   First of all, briefly examine the Mind Maps and Mini Mind Maps used in this book. What are the common characteristics? All of them use small pictures or symbols, with words branching out from the illustration.
2   Decide which idea or character in the book you want to illustrate and draw a picture, starting in the middle of the page so that you have plenty of room to branch out. Remember that no one expects a young Rembrandt or Picasso here; artistic ability is not as important as creating an image you (and you alone) will remember. A round smiling (or sad) face might work as well in your memory as a finished portrait. Use marking pens of different colors to make your Mind Map as vivid and memorable as possible.
3   As your thoughts flow freely, add descriptive works and other ideas on the colored branching lines that connect to the central image. Print clearly, using one word per line if possible.
4   Further refine your thinking by adding smaller branching lines, containing less important facts and ideas, to the main points.
5   Presto! You have a personal outline of your thoughts about the character and plot. It's not a stodgy formal outline, but a colorful image that will stick in your mind, it is hoped, throughout classroom discussions and final exams.

HOW TO READ A MIND MAP

1   Begin in the center, the focus of your topic.
2   The words/images attached to the center are like chapter headings; read them next.
3   Always read out from the center, in every direction (even on the left-hand side, where you will have to read from right to left, instead of the usual left to right).

USING MIND MAPS

Mind Maps are a versatile tool; use them for taking notes in class or from books, for solving problems, for brainstorming with friends, and for reviewing and working for tests or exams – their uses are endless. You will find them invaluable for planning essays for coursework and exams. Number your main branches in the order in which you want to use them and off you go – the main headings for your essay are done and all your ideas are logically organized.

Preparing for tests and exams

◆ Review your work systematically. Study hard at the start of your course, not the end, and avoid "exam panic"!
◆ Use Mind Maps throughout your course, and build a Master Mind Map for each subject – a giant Mind Map that summarizes everything you know about the subject.
◆ Use memory techniques such as mnemonics (verses or systems for remembering things like dates and events).
◆ Get together with one or two friends to study, compare Mind Maps, and discuss topics.

AND FINALLY...

Have *fun* while you learn – it has been shown that students who make their studies enjoyable understand and remember everything better and get the highest grades. I wish you and your brain every success!

(Tony Buzan)

HOW TO USE THIS GUIDE

This guide assumes that you have already read *To Kill a Mockingbird*, although you could read Background and The Story of *To Kill a Mockingbird* before that. It is best to use the guide alongside the text. You could read the Who's Who? and Themes sections without referring to the novel, but you will get more out of these sections if you do refer to it to check the points made in these sections, and especially when thinking about the questions designed to test your recall and help you think about the novel.

THE DIFFERENT SECTIONS

The Commentary section can be used in a number of ways. One way is to read a chapter or part of a chapter in the novel, and then read the commentary for that section. Continue until you come to a test yourself section – then take a break. Or, read the Commentary for a chapter or part of a chapter, then read that section in the novel, then go back to the Commentary. Find out what works best for you.

Topics for Discussion and Brainstorming gives topics that could well appear on exams or provide the basis for coursework. It would be particularly useful for you to discuss them with friends, or brainstorm them using Mind Map techniques (see p. vi).

How to Get an "A" in English Literature gives valuable advice on what to look for in a text, and what skills you need to develop in order to achieve your personal best.

The Exam Essay is a useful night-before reminder of how to tackle exam questions, and Model Answer and Essay Plan gives an example of an "A"-grade essay and the Mind Map and plan used to write it.

THE QUESTIONS

Whenever you come across a question in the guide with a star ✪ in front of it, think about it for a moment. You could even jot down a few words to focus your mind. There is not usually a "right" answer to these questions; it is important for you to develop your own opinions if you want to get an "A." The Test Yourself sections are designed to take you about 10–20 minutes each – which will be time well spent.

Key to icons

THEMES

A **theme** is an idea explored by an author. Whenever a theme is dealt with in the guide, the appropriate icon is used. This means you can find where a theme is mentioned just by flicking through the book. Try it now!

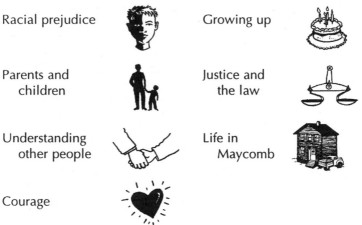

Racial prejudice

Growing up

Parents and children

Justice and the law

Understanding other people

Life in Maycomb

Courage

STYLE AND LANGUAGE

This heading and icon are used in the Commentary wherever there is a special section on the author's choice of words and **imagery** (a kind of word picture used to make an idea come alive).

BACKGROUND

The author

Nelle Harper Lee was born in Monroeville, Alabama, on April 28, 1926. Monroeville is a small southern town a bit like Maycomb in the novel. In some ways Harper Lee's life was like Scout's – indeed, many of her own experiences appear in the novel. Her father was a lawyer and she went to the local public schools. After that she studied law.

HOW THE BOOK WAS WRITTEN

Harper Lee gave up her law studies to become a writer. She took a job with an airline to earn money, and in 1957 sent some stories to a literary agent. She was encouraged to revise the stories and develop them. Harper Lee worked on this material for two and a half years, then sent in the story we now know as *To Kill a Mockingbird*. It was published in 1960.

HOW THE BOOK WAS RECEIVED

To Kill a Mockingbird was an immediate best-seller! It won the Pulitzer Prize for fiction, and in 1962 it was made into a film with Gregory Peck starring in the role of Atticus. Reviewers of the time praised the novel's authentic humor and its evocation of the world of childhood. Part of the reason for its success was that it coincided with the growth of the Civil Rights movement and presented ideas about equality and justice that were gaining more and more support. Then, as now, readers responded to the strong story and realistic, appealing characters.

The Historical Background

The incidents in *To Kill a Mockingbird* occurred in the United States at a time of economic hardships and widespread racial prejudice directed against African-Americans.

Following the crash of the stock market in 1929, America's Great Depression began. As conditions became worse, millions of people were out of work, and many were living in near starvation. When Franklin D. Roosevelt became president in 1933, he set up a variety of programs to provide employment and relieve the people of their terrible suffering.

Times were particularly hard in the southern part of the United States, a section that had not fully recovered from the aftermath of the Civil War. That war began when the southern states seceded from the Union, primarily over the issue of the right to own slaves, which was the basis of the South's economic prosperity.

At the time of *To Kill a Mockingbird,* many people in the South considered African-Americans inferior and continued to demand that they be segregated in separate schools and on trains and buses. Atticus Finch, a lawyer in the small Alabama town, was one of those who felt that the system of segregation was unfair and un-American.

THE STORY OF *TO KILL A MOCKINGBIRD*

The story is set in the 1930s in Maycomb, a small town in Alabama. The story is told by Scout Finch, who looks back to some important years in her childhood. Scout and her brother Jem were brought up by their father Atticus, a widower. Their African-American housekeeper, Calpurnia, helps Atticus with the children.

Scout starts school, and we learn about some of the local families, like the Cunninghams and the Ewells. We also learn a little about the educational system.

Scout, Jem, and their friend Dill, who visits every summer, are fascinated by their neighbor Boo Radley, who has stayed inside his house for fifteen years and is the subject of rumors and fear. They try a variety of strategies to make Boo come out of the house. Atticus, who is bringing up his children to respect and accept others as he does, disapproves of these activities. Jem and Scout find presents in the oak tree near their house. Jem realizes that they come from Boo. A fire burns down Miss Maudie's house and as the children watch, someone puts a blanket around Scout to keep her warm. They find out that the person was Boo.

Atticus is going to defend an African-American man, Tom Robinson, who has been accused of raping a white girl, Mayella Ewell. As a result the children hear their father criticized by a number of their racist neighbors, and even by members of their family. Atticus explains his reasons for wanting to take this case.

When a dog suffering from rabies threatens the safety of the town, Atticus is called on to shoot it. Atticus has hidden his talent for shooting from his children. He doesn't think a man with a gun is an example of true courage.

Jem is infuriated by the gibes of their neighbor, Mrs. Dubose, and cuts off the tops of her camellias. As a punishment he has to read to her every day for a month. When she dies, Atticus tells the children that Mrs. Dubose was a morphine addict who managed to give up her addiction before she died. She showed real courage.

The children visit Calpurnia's church and learn more about the African-American community and about the Tom Robinson case. Aunt Alexandra comes to stay and tries to impose her ideas about suitable behavior on the children and on Atticus.

As the Tom Robinson case comes to trial, Atticus is threatened for trying to protect him. Atticus's questioning in court makes it clear that Tom Robinson is innocent and that Mayella Ewell has been lying. In spite of the evidence the jury, after lengthy discussion, finds Tom guilty. Bob Ewell, the girl's father, threatens trouble for Atticus in the future. Tom Robinson tries to escape from prison and is shot seventeen times.

As Jem and Scout return from a Halloween pageant in the dark, Bob Ewell, armed with a knife, attacks them. Boo Radley leaves his house to save the children, and Bob Ewell is killed. To protect Boo, the sheriff persuades Atticus to accept the story that Bob Ewell fell on his knife.

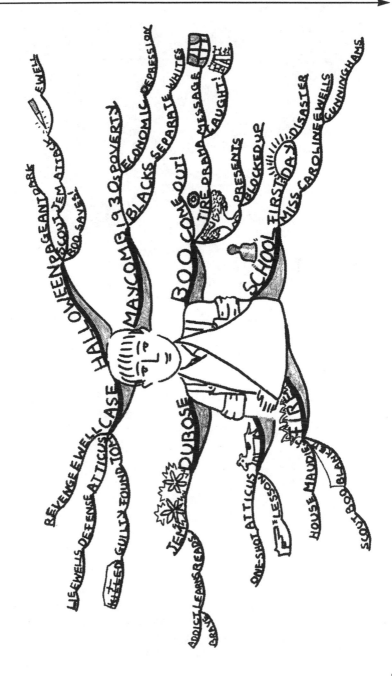

WHO'S WHO?

The Mini Mind Map above summarizes the main characters in *To Kill a Mockingbird*. Test yourself by looking at the full Mind Map on p. 11, then copy the Mini Mind Map and try to add to it from memory.

Atticus Finch

Atticus is a respected citizen of Maycomb, and the towns-people show their faith in him by consistently electing him to represent them on the state's legislative body. Atticus is named after a Roman who refused to take sides during the Roman civil war.

Atticus shows reason and tolerance, and teaches his children to see the other person's point of view. His compassion and humanity can be seen in the commitment with which he defends Tom Robinson and in his sympathy for Mayella Ewell. He is essentially civilized and gentle, qualities that are reflected in his declaration that *it's a sin to kill a mockingbird*.

Atticus shows courage in taking on Tom Robinson's defense. His is moral courage, which he teaches his children is far greater than being brave with a gun in your hand. Atticus's courage comes from his conviction that everyone is equal in the eyes of the law and from the necessity to follow his conscience. He has a strong sense of duty and integrity and knows that he would not be able to hold up his head in town if he did not live according to his principles.

Atticus is firm and fair with his children. He answers their questions honestly and insists on their behaving courteously. He has a keen sense of humor and shows them affection and respect.

Atticus's faith in human nature causes him to make some mistakes. He underestimates the lengths to which Bob Ewell will go to get his revenge, and he dismisses the idea that he might be in danger from a lynch mob.

Scout Finch

Scout is six years old when the story begins and nine when it ends. She is lively and impulsive, always ready to rush into a fight. She is quick-thinking and intelligent but, as Atticus says, doesn't use her head properly because she lets her emotions run away with her. Scout's undisciplined and unladylike behavior earns her Aunt Alexandra's criticism, and Scout resists her aunt's attempts to change her.

We see Scout trying to follow Atticus's instruction to fight with her "head" and not her fists. She gains self-control, and learns not to retaliate when she is taunted because Atticus is defending an African-American man. Her instinctive sympathy grows and develops as she learns to look at things from another person's point of view. We see this in the way she comes to understand Calpurnia, Aunt Alexandra, and Jem, and in her remorse at the end of the novel as she reflects on how their behavior must have affected Boo Radley. Scout's response to Boo here shows her sensitivity in the way she makes sure his public dignity is preserved as she walks him home.

Scout's natural warmth and friendliness are apparent in the way she behaves toward friends and neighbors. In the scene outside the jailhouse, these qualities diffuse a very ugly situation.

Jem Finch

Jem is ten when the story begins and thirteen when it finishes. During these years Jem goes through a painful process of growing up. At first he enjoys playing childish games with

Scout and Dill and relishes the fantasies about Boo Radley, but he becomes quieter and more reflective – moody, as Scout sees it – and develops compassion and understanding of Boo. He weeps when the hole in the tree is blocked up and becomes very upset about the prejudice and discrimination that characterize the world he lives in. Jem begins to identify himself as an adult, informing Atticus that Dill had run away from home and telling Scout how to behave toward Aunt Alexandra.

The trial has a huge effect on Jem. He is devastated by the verdict and finds it hard to come to terms with the depth of prejudice he encounters. His discussion of the trial shows his cleverness and intelligence, which are also seen in such incidents as his making the snowman out of dirt and snow. Jem's admiration and respect for Atticus grow throughout the book as he learns to appreciate the truly courageous nature of Atticus's work. He is similar to his father in his sensitivity and perseverance, as well as in his desire to be a lawyer.

We see the extent of Jem's growth in maturity after the trial, when Miss Maudie cuts him a slice from the grown-up cake, a symbolic gesture that acknowledges how far Jem has progressed in understanding and awareness.

Aunt Alexandra

Aunt Alexandra is Atticus's sister, but very unlike him. She has set ideas about the status of the Finch family and about the way Atticus should be bringing up Scout. Her snobbery and her prejudice alienate her from the tolerant Finches, but she fits in well with the rest of Maycomb.

Aunt Alexandra and our view of her change during the course of the novel. In spite of her opposition to Atticus, she does love him and is very concerned about the strain placed on him by the trial. She blames herself for the attack on Jem and Scout, and shows care and tenderness in the final crisis. Scout learns to admire the dignity and self-control that Aunt Alexandra shows when she goes back to the tea party after having heard of Tom's death.

Calpurnia

Calpurnia is firm with the children, slapping Scout when necessary and sharply reprimanding her, for example, when Scout was rude to Walter Cunningham at lunch. She is also kind and loving to them, especially to Scout, who relies on Cal for company when she is bored or lonely. Atticus trusts Cal with the care of his children and values her loyalty. He supports her when Aunt Alexandra is critical and says he couldn't do without her. Cal takes her responsibilities seriously, as we see when she storms down to the courtroom to report the children missing.

Calpurnia leads a double life. She is one of the few African-American in Maycomb who can read and write, but disguises her education when she is with her fellow African-Americans.

Dill

Dill comes to stay every summer with his Aunt Rachel. There is a suggestion that at other times he just gets passed around from relative to relative. Dill is a fragile and insecure character, who delights in make-believe and invention. His real life is unhappy. He feels his mother and stepfather have no time for him, but despite this he has lots of material possessions. Dill is sensitive and easily hurt. The outcome of the trial leaves him disillusioned and bewildered by the inhumanity people inflict on others. Dill's innocent wish to have babies with Scout and his admiration of Atticus show his longing for security and stability in a world that is fit only for clowns to laugh at.

Boo Radley

At the beginning of the story Boo Radley is a mysterious figure. There are stories that he poisons the pecan nuts in the school-yard and eats cats and squirrels raw. The children learn the truth about him, that he has been kept in solitary confinement since his youth because of a minor infringement of the law.

The children gradually learn that Boo is very different from the person they imagine him to be. He shows his concern and affection for them by a series of actions: putting little gifts in the oak tree, mending Jem's torn trousers when they get caught on the Radley fence, covering Scout with a blanket when she is watching the fire burn down Miss Maudie's house. Boo's final and greatest demonstration of his concern for the children is when he saves them from Bob Ewell's attack.

The children's growing maturity and understanding may be seen through their changing perception of Boo Radley. Boo is a solitary, innocent, kind person who, like the mockingbird, does no harm. He is the one who is harmed, mainly by the rigid pride of his family, who deny him full humanity.

Miss Maudie Atkinson

Miss Maudie is liked and respected by Jem and Scout. She lets them play in her garden, bakes them cakes, and is always straightforward and honest with them. Miss Maudie has no time for hypocrisy, and makes her feelings very clear. She speaks sharply to Mrs. Merriweather for criticizing Atticus, and mocks Stephanie Crawford for spreading rumors about Boo Radley. Miss Maudie is particularly critical of religious groups that claim to be Christian but whose behavior to others shows prejudice and lack of humanity.

In many ways Miss Maudie is like Atticus. She shares his lack of prejudice, his tolerance, and his courage, and, like him, she has a lively sense of humor. She finds the snowman amusing and yells back an answer to Uncle Jack's annual proposal across the street. Miss Maudie also shows hope when she explains to the children that a baby step has been taken along the road to a more tolerant future. Miss Maudie helps the children to understand their father. She tells them that his behavior is the same at home as on the public streets, and that he is civilized in his heart.

Miss Maudie is a sympathetic presence in the children's lives, and is a positive influence on their development. Her respect for life is reflected in her love for her garden and her plants, and her optimism may be seen in her calm acceptance of the loss of her house after the fire.

now that you know who's who, take a break

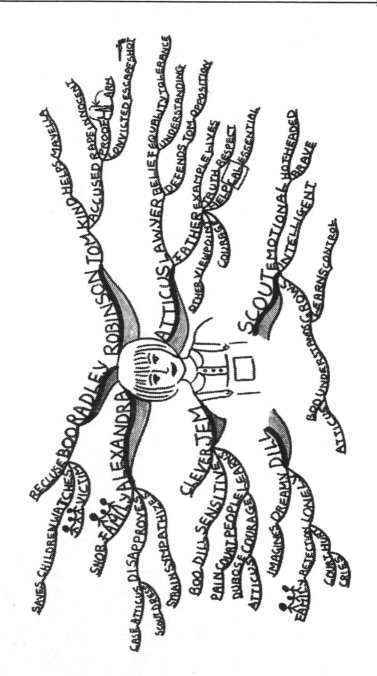

11

A theme is an idea developed or explored throughout a work. The Mini Mind Map above shows the main themes of *To Kill a Mockingbird*. Test yourself by copying the Mini Mind Map, adding to it, and then comparing your results with the version on p. 17.

Racial prejudice

The white and African-American communities are divided by deep-rooted fear and mistrust. As you will have read in the Background section, even after the end of slavery, the southern states did not change their attitude to the African-American people.

Poor white people, who would never have owned slaves before the Civil War, were particularly resentful of the newly free African-Americans, seeing them as a potential threat to their security. We see this in the bitter hatred expressed by Bob Ewell and by the lynch mob that sets out to kill Tom Robinson. The trial of Tom Robinson reveals the depths of the prejudice, which believes that African-American people are essentially inferior. Tom is clearly innocent of the crime of rape, but by his own admission is guilty of daring to feel sorry for a white woman. The white population could not accept such presumption.

The educated and better-off white families are less coarse and brutal in their attitude to the African-Americans, but still assume that they should keep their place. It is accepted that the African-Americans have their own living area and their own church, and that they should show deference to the whites. Look at the way the men take off their hats when Jem and Scout appear at church, and how the women make respectful gestures. Miss Gates complains that the "Negroes are getting above themselves," and the missionary circle speaks of "sulky, dissatisfied blacks." Even Scout says of Tom Robinson, when Dill is upset by his cross-examination, *after all, he's just a Negro.*

The characters who want change and plead for tolerance, such as Atticus and Miss Maudie, are seen as odd and non-conformist. The actions of people like Heck Tate and Judge Taylor show their commitment to justice and their lack of prejudice, but the process of change is painful and gradual. Think about how the African-Americans respond to Tom's trial and death. They are stirred up, but feel they have to accept it. The idea that they are inferior from birth is ingrained in both sections of the community, and a few decades will pass before any real change takes place.

Parents and children

Atticus shows his children love and respect. He does his best to bring them up to be rational, tolerant, and sensitive, and is disturbed when Alexandra criticizes his parenting. Aunt Alexandra acts as a kind of parent when she comes to stay for the period of the trial, and we can see the contrast between her ideas and those of Atticus. Calpurnia also is a kind of parent to Jem and Scout, and Atticus trusts her and is grateful to her for this role. Scout and Jem are fortunate in the adults who care for them. They learn something from each, and know they are loved.

Other children have less happy experiences. Bob Ewell is not a good parent. His children are filthy, unhealthy, and uneducated, and Burris is crude and foul-mouthed. Mayella's pathetic and ultimately dangerous attempts to bring some warmth into her deprived life show how much damage Bob

Ewell has inflicted. The Cunninghams are a contrast to the Ewells. Although the Cunningham children are poor and leave school when they are *field sized*, their family has pride and self-respect.

Dill and Boo Radley are also damaged children. Dill suffers from his parents' indifference and finds a substitute parent in Atticus. Boo's family are responsible for his confinement and his stunted development. Boo is a victim of his family's pride, isolation, and religious bigotry.

Understanding other people

One of the important messages in the book is that we will understand other people if we climb into their skin or walk in their shoes. Atticus teaches and reinforces this lesson throughout the book. The children come to understand Boo Radley, an understanding that is most movingly conveyed at the end of the novel when Scout literally stands in the position from which Boo has watched them and sees events as he will have seen them. They learn the truth about Dolphus Raymond and understand why he maintains his pretense of being a drunk. The idea of standing in the other person's shoes helps them to understand why the lynch mob turns away when Scout chats to Mr. Cunningham, and why Bob Ewell wants revenge.

Understanding other people is linked with the book's main image of the mockingbird. Tom Robinson and Boo Radley may be seen as mockingbird figures — they do no harm, but are persecuted and damaged by ignorance and prejudice. You will find more about the mockingbird image in the Style and Language sections in the Commentary.

Courage

We see different kinds of courage in the book. There are examples of physical courage, such as Atticus facing the rabid dog and Jem going back to get his trousers from the Radley fence. We also see moral courage, such as Atticus displays in taking on the case and sticking to his principles, even though he knows he cannot possibly win. Scout shows this kind of courage when she doesn't fight back when people criticize Atticus. Mrs. Dubose is such a strong example of someone with courage that Atticus calls her the bravest person he knows. She sets herself the goal of dying free from her drug addiction and achieves it with great effort. Atticus teaches the children that this, and not *a man with a gun in his hand,* is true courage.

Growing up

The main focus of growing up is on Scout and Jem. They become aware of changes within themselves. Some changes are physical, as in Jem's adolescent growth, and some have to do with understanding other people (see p. 14) and a growth in social and moral awareness. Part of growing up is learning more about people and society. The children have to learn about the prejudice that is *as much Maycomb as missionary teas,* and they discover the *simple hell people give other people.* In the process of growing up, the children learn the value of self-control, tolerance, and respect.

Justice and the law

According to the Declaration of Independence, *all men are created equal.* Atticus's deeply held belief is that this is undeniably true in a court of law; however, the operation of the law doesn't always lead to justice being done. As long as people are swayed and conditioned by prejudice, they will come to unjust decisions and verdicts. This is shown in the verdict against Tom. Atticus continues to have faith in the process of the law. The legal system could be improved, but what needs to change is the hearts and minds of people.

The other main representatives of the law are Judge Taylor and Heck Tate. Judge Taylor does his best to give Tom a fair trial by appointing Atticus and in the way he presides over the trial. Heck Tate's decision not to pursue the matter of Bob Ewell's death shows his belief in a natural justice that is more important than the letter of the law.

Life in Maycomb

Maycomb exhibits many of the values and attitudes of traditional southern culture, such as racial prejudice, social snobbery, and ingrained ideas about "family." Maycomb society is rigidly divided, and social status depends on family background. This idea is challenged by characters such as Miss Maudie, who declares that true background is decided by a person's moral worth.

Religion plays an important part in Maycomb life. Harper Lee attacks the hypocrites who speak about Christianity but mistreat their fellow human beings. The Baptists and the ladies of the missionary circle are particularly criticized for their lack of humanity.

Women in Maycomb society are expected to conform to traditional ideas about southern femininity. Scout accepts the fact that eventually she will have to conform, and comes to recognize some value in the code of feminine behavior displayed by ladies like Aunt Alexandra.

Education is also criticized by Harper Lee. The school system and the lessons the children receive are gently mocked. The children learn lessons of real value from other sources, and the attitudes displayed by their teacher are opposed to the humanitarian ideas of the book.

time for a breather before we tackle the Commentary

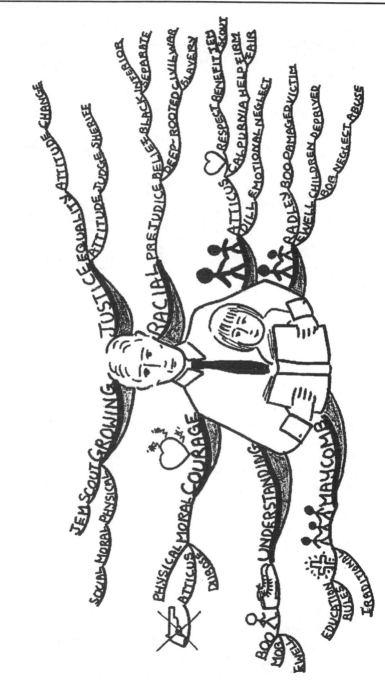

17

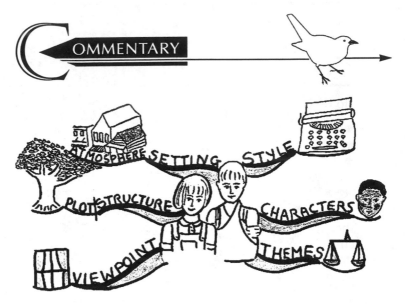

COMMENTARY

The Commentary divides the chapters into short sections, beginning with a brief preview that will prepare you for the section and help with last-minute review. The Commentary comments on whatever is important in the section, focusing on the areas shown in the Mini Mind Map above.

ICONS

Wherever there is a focus on a particular theme, the icon for that theme appears in the margin (see p. x for key). Look out, too, for the Style and Language sections. Being able to comment on style and language will help you to get an "A" on your exam.

You will learn more from the Commentary if you use it alongside the novel itself. Read a section from the novel, then the corresponding Commentary section – or the other way around.

QUESTIONS

Remember that whenever a question appears in the Commentary with a star ✪ in front of it, you should stop and think about it for a moment. And do **remember to take a break** after completing each exercise.

Chapter 1

The start of it all

(To *Our father said we were both right*.)

◆ Scout begins to tell the story.
◆ She looks back to when Jem was nearly thirteen.
◆ Jem thinks the story begins the summer when Dill arrived.

There are two important points to be aware of at the beginning of the novel: first, Scout is the first-person narrator who tells the story from her point of view; second, she is looking back at events that happened when she was a child. ❂ What do you think are the advantages of telling a story through a child's eyes? Can you think of any disadvantages?

Atticus and the Finch family

(From *Being Southerners*, to *nearly every family in town*.)

◆ The Finch clan was established by Simon Finch over a hundred years ago.
◆ He founded the family homestead, Finch's Landing.
◆ Atticus left to study law in Montgomery, then moved to Maycomb to practice law.
◆ Atticus's brother studied medicine at Boston, with financial help from Atticus.
◆ Atticus's sister Alexandra stayed at Finch's landing.

We see how important family background and family characteristics are in this society. Notice how the Haverfords are classified as stupid and stubborn. ❂ What do you think about putting people in categories in this way? Maycomb is a community where everyone knows everyone else, with a population that changes very little.

![Your assignment]

? Take ten minutes to think about the place where the novel is set. Look at the map below showing part of the state of Alabama. Decide where you think the town of Maycomb is. Write it in. Write in the names of the characters who live in the places marked.

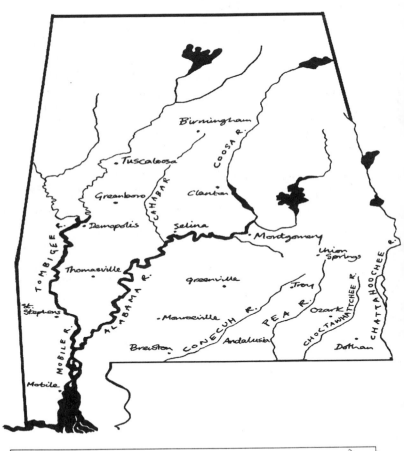

Dill's arrival

(From *Maycomb was an old town*, to *the idea of making Boo Radley come out*.)

◆ We find out that Atticus's wife (Jem and Scout's mother) died when Scout was two.

◆ Calpurnia, the family's African-American cook, has looked after them since then.

◆ Dill comes to spend the summer with his Aunt Rachel.

Scout's description of Maycomb makes us see a small, tired town, where life is slow and little happens. This is the period of the Depression in America, when the South in particular suffered great poverty. There is only a vague hope that the newly elected President, Franklin D. Roosevelt, will help things to improve.

Scout says that Calpurnia is *tyrannical* with a wide and hard hand. ✪ What does this tell you about the way Calpurnia treats her? Does Atticus share Scout's view of Calpurnia?

Dill is only seven, but he earns the children's respect and acceptance because he has seen films like *Dracula,* and his lively imagination is a great asset in their make-believe games. Note how Dill reacts when Scout asks about his father. ✪ Is Dill lying when he says he hasn't got one? Why does he reply like this?

Boo and the Radleys

(From *The Radley Place fascinated Dill,* to *and he drooled most of the time.*)

◆ The Radleys have always kept to themselves.

◆ Arthur (Boo) Radley got in with the wrong crowd in his teens, and got into trouble.

◆ His father told the judge he would keep Arthur out of trouble in the future.

◆ He isolated Boo within the house.

◆ Boo is now looked after in the same way by his elder brother, Nathan.

◆ There are many stories and rumors about Boo Radley.

The people of Maycomb regard the Radleys as strange because they don't behave as the rest of the community does. They don't visit neighbors or join in local activities. The

Radley Place and its mysterious inhabitant are looked at with fear and superstition. ✪ From what you know about Maycomb, are you surprised that they react like this? We see the importance of religion to this community. Going to church is Maycomb's *principal recreation*; Mr. Radley *took the word of God as his only law*; the only films ever shown are *Jesus ones*. ✪ Does religion influence the way characters behave toward each other? What do you think is the author's view of religion as practiced in Maycomb?

Mr. Radley's way of keeping his son out of trouble is to keep him away from the outside world. ✪ What do you think of the way he treats his son? We see what Calpurnia thinks when she calls him the meanest man who ever lived. African-American people rarely comment on white people's behavior. ✪ What does this tell you about the relationship between African-Americans and whites?

Atticus tells Jem that the Radleys have a right to be left alone and that Boo isn't kept chained to a bed, that there were *other ways of making people into ghosts*. ✪ What do you think Atticus means?

"Just go up and touch the house"

(From "*Let's try to make him come out*," to the end of the chapter.)

◆ Dill wants to make Boo Radley come out of the house.
◆ Dill dares Jem to knock on the Radley front door.
◆ Eventually, Dill reduces the dare to just touching the house, and Jem does it.
◆ The children think they see a movement at one of the windows.

Jem is scared of the Radley Place, but it is a point of honor with him not to turn down a dare. Dill taunts him with being afraid, like all the people in Maycomb, but Jem still hesitates and makes excuses. Scout's sneer makes him do it in the end. Notice the way Harper Lee makes the children's private world vivid and realistic through the way they speak and react to each other.

Test yourself

? See how much you have learned about Maycomb and about Boo Radley.
Look at these words and put a circle around the ones that describe Maycomb.

dynamic	lively	conservative	slow
conventional	superstitious	cautious	
judgmental	tolerant	prejudiced	
open-minded	scared	self-righteous	

? Look at these statements about Boo Radley and check off the ones that are true.
- Boo Radley poisons chickens and household pets.
- When Boo Radley was in his teens he was sent to the state industrial school.
- When Boo was thirty-three he attacked his father with a pair of scissors.
- Mr. Radley kept Boo chained to the bed.
- Boo frightened Rachel Crawford by looking at her through her window.
- Boo has yellow teeth and a long, jagged scar.
- Boo wasn't seen for fifteen years.

now take a break before reading about Scout being punished for bad behavior

Chapter 2

That damn lady!

(To *I seldom pleased her and she seldom rewarded me.*)

◆ Dill goes home and Scout starts school.
◆ Scout gets into trouble with the new teacher, Miss Caroline Fisher.
◆ Miss Caroline is annoyed because Scout can already read and write.

Scout looks forward to starting school, but is quickly disillusioned. Her relationship with Jem begins to change, as Jem is condescending toward her and says that their home life is to be kept separate from school.

Notice the way Miss Caroline is seen as an outsider, because she comes from the northern part of the state, which tried to remain neutral during the Civil War and is more industrial than the southern part of Alabama. ✪ Are the children likely to have formed these views for themselves? Whose ideas influence them? The Civil War has been over for more than sixty years. ✪ What does this tell you about Maycomb?

Miss Caroline has fixed ideas about how to teach and cannot adapt them to suit the individuals in her class. She reads the class a story about cats that is totally unsuitable for the children, who are mainly from poor farming families. She is unprepared for the fact that Scout can already read and write and shows her displeasure at this. ✪ What do you think about Miss Caroline's reaction here? What could the author be suggesting about the educational system?

Scout can't understand what she has done wrong. She can't remember ever not being able to read. Reading is an activity she associates with Atticus, with crawling into his lap every night and looking at whatever he is reading. ✪ What does this tell you about Scout's feelings for her father?

Calpurnia helped to develop Scout's competence at writing by supplying Scout with (setting) her tasks to keep her occupied and rewarding her if she has copied them satisfactorily. ✪ How is Calpurnia's contribution to Scout's education different from that of Atticus? Does Scout appreciate her help?

Walter and the Cunninghams

(From *Everybody who goes home to lunch*, to the end of the chapter.)

◆ Miss Caroline offers to lend Walter Cunningham some lunch money.
◆ Scout has to explain that the Cunninghams don't accept anything they can't pay back.

◆ Miss Caroline punishes Scout by hitting her hand with a ruler and making her stand in the corner.

Notice the way Scout tries to explain to Miss Caroline that the Cunninghams are proud and independent, unwilling to accept charity. Because everyone in Maycomb knows this, she assumes that Miss Caroline will too. Scout understands that the Cunninghams are poor but make do with what they have. Like many farmers at the time, poverty has forced them to sign an *entailment*. This is a legal term that means that land is settled on a number of people so that no one individual is its absolute owner. As a result, the Cunninghams have little actual cash. They pay for Atticus's legal services with goods from their land. ❂ Look at the description of Walter. What details show that he is poor? What details show that he has some personal pride?

At the end of the morning, Miss Caroline buries her head in her arms. ❂ What do you think she is feeling? Do you feel sorry for her? Are her problems all her own fault?

Over to you

? Scout's account of her first morning at school tells us something about the education system, the poverty experienced by farmers in the South, and the difficulties faced by an outsider in Maycomb. Start a Mind Map describing Scout's first day. Try to include points in favor of Miss Caroline as well as points against her.

STYLE AND LANGUAGE

You will have noticed that, although the story is told from a child's point of view, the language is not the restricted language of a six-year-old. That is because the book is written by the adult Scout, looking back and recreating the events of her childhood. Some of the book's humor arises from the contrast between Scout's childish innocence and the adult perspective. Examples of this can be found in her comments about Calpurnia and in the freshness and naïveté of her explanations to Miss Caroline.

Chapter 3

A dinner drowned in syrup

(To "and you mind her, you hear?")

◆ Walter has dinner with the Finches.
◆ Scout is scolded for her bad manners.

Scout blames Walter for getting her into trouble. She gets him on the ground and rubs his nose in the dirt. ✪ What do you think about this way of expressing feelings? Why does Jem stop her? We see Scout mocking Jem's boasts about how brave he is. Find some more examples of Scout doing this in Chapter 1. Notice the way we see the affection between Jem and Scout even as they tease and criticize each other.

Scout blurts out her horror when Walter pours syrup all over his food. Notice the way Atticus silently reprimands her. ✪ Why doesn't Atticus say something to Scout about her behavior? Calpurnia calls Scout into the kitchen and tells her off for being rude to a guest. She teaches Scout that everyone is entitled to respect, courtesy, and tolerance. ✪ Are you surprised that Scout is furious with Cal for this? Atticus tells Scout how important Cal is to the family. What detail shows he is angry with Scout? Can you think of some words to describe how Atticus sees Calpurnia?

Burris and the Ewells

(From I returned to school, to made me think of running away.)

◆ Miss Caroline discovers a cootie (a louse) in Burris Ewell's hair.
◆ Burris Ewell is abusive and threatening to Miss Caroline.
◆ The class explains about the Ewells and comforts the teacher.

Burris Ewell is the filthiest person Scout has ever seen. The only clean part of him is a fist-sized space on his face.
✪ What does this detail suggest to you? Miss Caroline learns that the Ewells attend school for the first day of

the year only, and that Burris is known to be mean and dangerous. ❂ What do you think about the way the class treats Miss Caroline when she is upset?

"Climb into his skin"

(From *By late afternoon*, to the end of the chapter.)

◆ Calpurnia is kind to Scout.
◆ Scout tells Atticus she doesn't want to go back to school.
◆ Atticus teaches Scout to look at things from the other person's point of view.
◆ Atticus gets Scout to agree that she will go back to school if they continue to read every night.

We have another example here of Scout seeing things from her own point of view. She thinks that Cal is being kind to her because she is secretly sorry for her harsh treatment of Scout.

The idea that you should climb into another person's skin and see things from his or her point of view is a major theme in the book. Atticus teaches Scout this most important lesson when he asks her to see the day's events from Miss Caroline's point of view. (You might like to add to your Mind Map of Chapter 2 at this point.) Atticus also helps Scout to understand why the Ewells are treated differently from other people. The family is *the disgrace of Maycomb*, living like animals in filth and disease. Bob Ewell gets away with breaking the law for the sake of his children. ❂ What does this tell you about the Maycomb community?

Test yourself

? You have learned something about two poor white families, the Cunninghams and the Ewells. Begin a Mind Map showing the similarities and differences between them.

? Think about the kind of father Atticus is. You could jot down some ideas, or begin a Mind Map of Atticus with "father" as one of the branches.

? Below is a timeline to help you to track the main events in the novel. It has been started for you. Fill in the important happenings and people so far. Use signs and symbols as well as words.

1933   1935

Summer   September   October

time for a break before going on to hear about some mysterious presents and a dramatic production.

✎ STYLE AND LANGUAGE

Harper Lee uses a variety of language to show different characters, and to create humor. The children have a distinctive way of speaking. They use slang, dialect, and colloquial expressions that vividly capture their speech rhythms and interactions. Atticus, on the other hand, uses what Scout calls *last-will-and-testament diction*. His way of speaking reveals his legal background. He speaks formally and sometimes dryly, and doesn't make concessions when speaking to the children. They ask him to explain any words they don't understand. An example of the humorous effect of Atticus's language is when he refers to the children's custom of spitting to seal a promise as *the usual formality*.

Language is also used for satirical effect, as when Miss Caroline, comforted by the class's concern, *mystified* the first grade with a story about a "toadfrog" that lived in a hall.

Chapter 4

Gifts in the oak tree

(To *and I folded myself inside the tire.*)

◆ Scout finds chewing gum in the oak tree.
◆ Jem and Scout find two pennies in the oak tree.
◆ Dill arrives for the summer.

A year has passed, and Scout is frustrated and bored with school. ❍ From which sources do you think Scout receives her real education?

Jem's strong reaction when Scout chews the gum she found in the tree shows his continued superstitious fear of the Radley Place. He is more thoughtful when they find the Indian head pennies, and we see him gazing at the Radley place and thinking. ❍ Do you think Jem is beginning to connect the gifts with Boo Radley? Has Scout made this connection?

Look at the stories Dill tells about his journey from Meridian. ❍ Do you think they are true? Do you think he is telling the truth about his father?

A town like Maycomb

Over to you

? Take ten minutes to think about the important places in Maycomb. Use the information you have gained to add to the illustration on p. 29: the Finch household, the Radley Place, the school, Mrs. Dubose's house.

"One Man's Family"

(From *Until it happened* to the end of the chapter.)

◆ Scout rolls inside a tire into the Radley garden.
◆ Jem has to get the tire back.
◆ The children invent a new game, turning the story of Boo Radley into a play.
◆ Atticus shows his disapproval of this game.

Scout's frightening roll in the tire is dramatically presented. We see her suffocating as the surroundings melt into *a mad palette*. Jem's panic when she is popped out onto Radley ground is shown in the way he *yelled* and *hollered*. He is terrified of having to go on to Radley ground to get the tire back, but acts like a hero once he has. Jem's idea of playing Boo Radley is another way of showing he isn't afraid of the Radleys, unlike Scout. He thinks Scout wants to drop the game because she's a coward. ✪ What are the two reasons for Scout wanting to finish the game?

A recap

? Spend ten minutes gathering your ideas about Scout and Jem. During the book they grow in maturity and in their understanding of other people. Look at the tree on p. 31 and the events that bring each of them closer to this maturity and understanding. You could use signs and pictures as well as words.

meet an eccentric neighbor and see how a fishing pole gets the children into trouble – after the break.

The Tree of Understanding: mark Jem's and Scout's progress

Chapter 5

Miss Maudie's porch

(To *I liked it very much.*)

◆ Jem and Dill spend a lot of time together.
◆ Scout turns to Miss Maudie for company.
◆ Miss Maudie tells Scout more about the Radleys and about Atticus.

An advantage of Scout's exclusion from the boys' activities is that she gets to know Miss Maudie better. Miss Maudie is always kind to the children, generously allowing them the use of her garden and baking them three little cakes. They like her because she is straight with them and they can trust her. Miss Maudie's sharp, down-to-earth approach to life cuts through gossip and rumors about Boo. Notice the way she tells Scout that Boo is alive, but refuses to indulge her by rehashing the details of what happened to him. ✿ What do you think of the way Miss Maudie dealt with Stephanie Crawford's story about Boo?

Miss Maudie is sympathetic to Boo because he is the victim of his father's religious bigotry. Miss Maudie is scathing about the Baptists, the religious group old Mr. Radley belonged to. She thinks their practice of interpreting the Bible literally is dangerous, and dislikes their attitude to pleasure and to women. We see Harper Lee's dislike of intolerance and hypocrisy through Miss Maudie's ideas. ✿ Do you understand Boo's situation more than you did at the beginning of the book?

Miss Maudie likes and admires Atticus because he is not hypocritical. Atticus's behavior is consistent with his principles.

Your turn

? Rate the characters below according to their degree of tolerance and understanding of others. Put the one you think shows the most tolerance at the top, and work down:

Scout, Jem, Miss Maudie, Miss Caroline, Atticus, old Mr. Radley, Stephanie Crawford.

? Add to your Mind Map of Atticus.

Asking Boo to come out

(From *Next morning when I awakened*, to the end of the chapter.)

◆ The children try to push a letter to Boo through the window.
◆ Atticus catches them and tells them to leave Boo alone.

Scout is horrified at the thought of giving a note to Boo Radley, in spite of Miss Maudie's words. She reluctantly agrees to join in the plot. ❂ What is she going to say when she tells Jem that *somebody was ____*?

Atticus is very firm in his insistence that the children stop tormenting Boo Radley. He asks them to consider Boo's point of view and and to respect his right to live as he chooses. Notice the way Atticus tricks Jem into revealing that the game Atticus has seen them playing was based on Boo's life. Jem sees this as a lawyer's trick and is angry that he let himself fall for it. ❂ Why does Jem wait until Atticus is out of earshot before yelling at him?

Dill continues to make up stories about his life. Scout is very quick to spot inconsistencies, such as Dill's remark that his father doesn't have a beard. ❂ Why does Dill make up these things? What does Scout think about his inventions?

Think about

? What have you gathered so far about Dill's character and the kind of life he has? Draw a Mind Map to show your thoughts and ideas.

in the next chapter the children make a final attempt to contact Boo. Have a break first

Chapter 6

The roar of a shotgun

(To *he bawled after us.*)

◆ On Dill's last night in Maycomb, the children try to look at Boo through a window.

◆ They see a man's shadow and hear a shotgun.

◆ They escape, but Jem loses his trousers on barbed wire.

◆ Nathan Radley tells the neighbors he shot a black man on his property.

◆ Dill comes up with an excuse for Jem's trousers being missing

Scout joins in this plan only when Jem taunts her that she is getting more like a girl every day. ❍ When else has Jem said this? Why is it regarded as an insult?

The story is told from a white person's point of view, and so far there has been little reference to the African-American community (apart from Calpurnia). Notice what Nathan Radley says about the intruder in his collard patch. ❍ What does this tell you about the position of African-Americans in Maycomb?

Dill's gift for invention keeps the children out of trouble for being on the Radley property. The adults' attention is deflected from the Radley Place as they reprimand the children for gambling.

❍ Think about Dill's *engagement* to Scout, and the way he gives her a kiss and reminds her to write. How does Dill see the Finch family? You might want to add to your Mind Map of Dill at this point.

Jem gets his pants back

(From *Had Jem's pants*, to the end of the chapter.)

◆ Later that night, Jem goes back to get his trousers.

The experience in the Radley garden has terrified Scout. Notice the way she imagines an insane Boo coming

after them to get revenge. Scout tries to prevent Jem from going back to get his trousers; she says it would be better to face Atticus's anger than Nathan Radley's shotgun. Jem would rather risk getting caught or shot than disappointing Atticus. ◎ What differences do you find in Jem's relationship with Atticus and Scout's?

This incident marks a turning point in Jem's and Scout's relationship. Scout finds it impossible to understand why Jem won't tell Atticus the truth. ◎ Do you understand Jem's feelings?

STYLE AND LANGUAGE

The tense atmosphere as the children enter the Radley Place is effectively created. We see the children moving quietly and stealthily, and jump when we hear the gate and the bottom step squeak. The back of the Radley house is unfamiliar and eerie, and the observation of the stove and the hat rack gives it a frightening reality. There is a rush of fear as the shadow appears. The simile *crisp as toast* heightens our awareness of its threatening presence. We see the children's panic in words like *leaped, galloped, flung,* and *dived,* which suggest headlong movement. Notice the contrast between this section and the humor of children's deliberately casual approach to the group of neighbors and the moment when they realize Jem doesn't have his trousers on.

Over to you

? Add to your tree on p. 31. Who has climbed the further? You could also add to your Mind Map of Atticus.

now relax for a minute before going on to find out about Jem's torn trousers, more gifts in the tree, and why they will be the last

Chapter 7

Mended trousers

(To *even I can't tell sometimes.*)

◆ Jem tells Scout that his trousers had been mended and folded for him.

Notice the way Scout tries to understand Jem's moodiness by applying Atticus's advice and climbing into his skin. She assumes that Jem is suffering the aftereffects of the frightening experience of collecting his trousers. When she is told about them, Scout doesn't see the significance of the repaired trousers. We see how Jem's understanding and awareness is developing more fully than the younger Scout's. ✪ What does Jem feel about Boo leaving his trousers for him?

More gifts in the oak tree

(From *We were walking past our tree*, to *Jem put the note in an envelope*.)

◆ The children find twine, soap carvings of two figures, chewing gum, a medal, and a watch.
◆ Jem writes a thank-you letter to put in the tree.

We see Jem gradually understanding and accepting that the gifts in the tree come from Boo. He realizes that the dolls have been carved by someone who has studied the children's appearance. He asks Atticus about the spelling medal, trying to find out whom it might belong to. Jem's decision to thank the mysterious giver shows his sensitivity and his growing awareness of the other person. ✪ How is Jem's perception of Boo Radley changing?

Blocked up

(From *Next morning*, to the end of the chapter.)

◆ Jem tries to put the letter in the tree, but the hole is blocked up with cement.

◆ Jem realizes that Nathan Radley blocked the hole to cut off communication with the children.

Jem shows concern for Scout when he asks her not to cry. Notice the way he asks questions to find out the truth about the tree, courageously approaching Nathan Radley, then checking his reply with Atticus. Jem is moved to tears when he realizes that Nathan Radley has deliberately prevented Boo from showing friendship to the children. ❂ What do you think Jem is feeling about Boo at this point? What might he be feeling about the way he has behaved toward Boo in the past? Notice that Scout has not made the same connections as Jem. ❂ Why is this, do you think?

Think about

? You will want to add to your Tree at this point. You could also fill in more of your Timeline.

? Gather together your ideas about Boo Radley. Think about the things you know are true, the things you know are rumors, and the things you can piece together from the story. Describe your ideas in a Mind Map.

? Try this way of remembering the items left in the oak tree:

Gum
Indian head pennies
Figures
Twine

time for a break. There's snow and fire to come.

Chapter 8

Fun and disaster

(To *I shuddered when Atticus started a fire in the kitchen stove.*)

◆ The children see snow for the first time.
◆ They make a snowman.
◆ Miss Maudie's house burns down.
◆ The children watch the fire from in front of the Radley Place.

 Scout's response to the snow is amusing. Never having experienced it before, she thinks it's the end of the world! She helps Jem to build a snowman, and they have great fun making it look first like Mr. Avery, then like a mixture of Mr. Avery and Miss Maudie (to avoid offending Mr. Avery). The fun turns to drama as the fire starts and the town is alerted to deal with it.

We are aware of the town's smallness and its isolation. Notice how many jobs the one telephone operator does and how they have to get help from Abbotsville and Clark's Ferry because the old Maycomb fire truck breaks down.

A blanket from Boo

(From *As we drank our cocoa,* to the end of the chapter.)

◆ Atticus notices a blanket around Scout's shoulders.
◆ Jem realizes Boo must have put it on her.
◆ Jem pours out his thoughts about Boo and Nathan Radley.
◆ Miss Maudie accepts the loss of her house.

Notice the difference in the children's reaction to Boo covering Scout with the blanket. Jem becomes nearly hysterical as he tells Atticus that he mustn't send the blanket back because Nathan mustn't know about Boo's action. Jem knows now that Boo is not dangerous, but kind and thoughtful to them. Jem had moved from fearing Boo to being protective of him. ✪ What about Scout? Does she understand what Jem says? Which words tell us how Scout still sees Boo?

You will have noticed how Miss Maudie's love of her garden is a linking theme through the book. We have been told in Chapter 5 that she loved everything that grew in God's earth, and that she was criticized by the strict Baptists for her love of flowers. The blaze that destroys her house was started by a fire she lit to keep her potted plants warm. Miss Maudie accepts the loss of her home, and views the future optimistically. Her concern is for the neighborhood. ❍ Which of these characters is Miss Maudie most like: Miss Caroline, Rachel Haverford, Mr. Avery, Atticus, or Nathan Radley? Give reasons for your choice.

 *STYLE AND LANGUAGE*

The description of the fire is effectively conveyed. At first it is heard: *soft taffeta-like sounds and muffled scurrying sounds.* The repetition of "s" makes us hear the sound and sense the movement of the flames. The word *spewing* shows the force of the flame that comes from Miss Maudie's window. We hear the wail of the fire siren and the spurting water on the pavement as the hose bursts. We see the denseness of the smoke in the simile, *Smoke was rolling off our house....like fog off a river bank.* The picture of men working in their pajama tops and nightshirts helps to convey the sense of panic and danger.

Your turn

?   Add to your Timeline and your Mind Map of Boo.

Chapter 9

"I'm simply defending a Negro"

(To *Then Christmas came and disaster struck.*)

◆ Atticus explains to Scout why he is defending Tom Robinson.
◆ Atticus tells Scout to be ready for insults and criticism.
◆ He asks her not to respond by fighting.

Atticus tells Scout that defending Tom Robinson is a matter of conscience and principle for him. He has to take the case for the sake of his self-respect, even though he knows he can't win. ✪ Why is Atticus sure he will lose? What have you gathered about the position of African-Americans in the southern states?

Atticus warns Scout that they will be fighting their friends, but he wants her to fight with her head (not literally of course!) instead of her fists. Scout tries to change, and walks away from a fight for the first time. ✪ Do you think she will find it easy to continue like this?

Christmas at Finch's Landing

(From *Jem and I viewed Christmas with mixed feelings*, to *so I didn't hear him*.)

◆ Atticus and the children go to stay with Aunt Alexandra, Uncle Jack, and Cousin Francis.
◆ Scout is criticized for being unladylike.

Scout dislikes her cousin Francis; they have nothing in common, he is boring, and he tells tales to Aunt Alexandra. She feels no warmth for Aunt Alexandra, who hurts Scout's feelings with her critical attitude. Scout likes Uncle Jack, who is warm and funny, although he doesn't understand children.

Uncle Jack and Aunt Alexandra think that Atticus is too lenient with the children. Atticus ignores Scout's swearing, knowing that she's looking for attention and will grow out of it, and he doesn't mind Scout wearing *unladylike* clothes. ✪ What do you think of the way Atticus is bringing up Jem and Scout? What kind of behavior does he get angry with them about?

Scout realizes that there are fixed ideas about how females (and males) in the South should look and behave. Scout doesn't want to conform to the stereotype, and rejects Aunt Alexandra's opinion that she should wear dresses and feminine trinkets and play house.

The attack on Francis

(From *Francis sat beside me on the back steps*, to *but he made no sense whatsoever*.)

◆ Francis is rude about Dill and criticizes Atticus.
◆ Scout hits Francis and Francis lies about the incident.
◆ Scout tells Uncle Jack her side of the story.

 Francis calls Dill *a little runt* and says that he's passed around from relative to relative. ✪ Do you think there's a connection between Dill's lack of security and his fascination with Boo Radley? Scout takes this, but explodes when Francis calls Atticus a *nigger-lover* and says he is disgracing the family. ✪ Are you surprised that Scout reacts like this?

Scout is angry with Uncle Jack for not listening to her version of what happened. ✪ What does Atticus do when Jem and Scout fight? When Scout asks Uncle Jack what a *whore-lady* is, he avoids answering the question. ✪ How does Atticus deal with the children's questions? Scout asks Uncle Jack not to tell Atticus what the fight was about. ✪ What does this tell you about Scout's feelings for her father?

Maycomb's usual disease

(From *later, when I was supposed to be in bed*, to the end of the chapter.)

◆ Scout overhears Atticus and Uncle Jack talking.
◆ Atticus says he is worried about how Scout will deal with the trial.
◆ Atticus wants Jem and Scout to trust him and to go to him for answers.
◆ Years later Scout realizes that Atticus wanted her to hear.

When Atticus realizes Scout is listening to his conversation with Uncle Jack, he begins to talk about the trial. Both children are in for some ugly incidents in the coming months. Atticus doesn't worry about Jem keeping his head, but he does worry about how Scout will handle the kind of abuse and criticism she will encounter. ✪ Is Atticus right to worry about Scout and not Jem?

Once again we realize that Atticus cannot possibly win this case, because the word of a black man will not be believed against the word of a white man. He calls prejudice against black people *Maycomb's usual disease,* and hopes that his children won't be influenced by it. Atticus is one of the few people in Maycomb who don't have the *disease* of prejudice. ✪ Start to make a note of any people who share the same views as Atticus.

Over to you

❓ Spend ten minutes on your Mind Map of Atticus. Some branches could include: lawyer, neighbor, brother.

take a short break. There's a mad dog in the next chapter!

Chapter 10

"It's a sin to kill a mockingbird"

(To *make touchdowns for the Baptists.*)

◆ Scout and Jem express their disappointment that Atticus isn't like the other fathers.

Atticus is different from the children's friends' parents. He is older than most of them, and he doesn't enjoy the same sporting and recreational activities, preferring reading to other pastimes. As Scout sees it, his job isn't one to inspire admiration. Physically Atticus seems frail. His eyesight is poor, and he won't play football.

Atticus accepts that the children will shoot birds with their new air rifles, although he would rather they didn't. He instructs them not to kill mockingbirds. Miss Maudie explains that mockingbirds do no harm, but just give pleasure. ✪ Which people in the book are like mockingbirds?

Ol' One-Shot

(From *One Saturday Jem and I decided*, to the end of the chapter.)

◆ A rabid dog approaches the house.
◆ Atticus kills it with a single shot.

The children are amazed when the sheriff, Heck Tate, hands the rifle to Atticus to shoot the dog. Atticus has not told the children about his marksmanship. When Jem realizes that his father was the best shot in Maycomb County, he can hardly speak for his pride and confusion. Notice that once again it is Miss Maudie who interprets Atticus for the children and helps them to understand him. She explains that Atticus chose not to exercise his talent for shooting unless he had to, because it gave him an unfair advantage over living things. ○ What do you think of Atticus's decision?

We see the difference between Jem's and Scout's level of understanding. Jem is elated by the realization that his father is not only good with a gun, but *civilized in his heart* and a *gentleman*. Scout sees only her father's talent, and wants to boast about it. ○ How has Jem's understanding of his father grown?

Your turn

? It's time now to note your impressions of Miss Maudie. What is she like, and what is her function in the novel? (Think about the different ways she helps the children.) You can put your ideas in a Mind Map.

? Remember to add to your Mind Map of Atticus, and your Tree!

STYLE AND LANGUAGE

This is the first time in the book that we meet the mockingbird symbol. A symbol in literature is something a writer uses to stand for or suggest something else. The mockingbird in this chapter suggests innocence and goodness. As the book's title says, it would be a sin to kill a creature that does no harm. The mockingbird also symbolizes a world that is free from fear or evil. You will notice throughout the book that when we are told the mockingbirds fall silent, something ugly or dangerous is about to happen. ❷ Can you find the place in this chapter where the mockingbirds are quiet?

Chapter 11

Jem loses his head

(To *Just pretend you're inside the Radley house.*)

◆ Mrs. Dubose insults the children and Atticus.
◆ Jem loses his temper and cuts off the tops of Mrs. Dubose's camellia bushes.
◆ Atticus is angry and sends Jem to talk to Mrs. Dubose.
◆ Atticus talks to Scout about the Tom Robinson case.

 The children hate their elderly neighbor Mrs. Dubose because she has a vicious tongue and hurls insults at them. Atticus tells Jem to hold his head high and be a gentleman, but when Mrs. Dubose insults Atticus for defending Tom Robinson, Jem can't control his anger. Jem is usually easygoing. ❷ Why does he react so strongly here?

Atticus explains to Scout that he has to do what he thinks is right, even if other people disagree with him. As a matter of conscience, he has to take the Tom Robinson case. ❷ Do you think Atticus is right to defend Tom Robinson? He knows he won't win and that the children will have more unpleasant experiences. Should Atticus have refused to take the case?

Real courage

(From *The following Monday afternoon*, to the end of the chapter.)

◆ Jem has to read to Mrs. Dubose for a month, for a few minutes longer every day.
◆ Mrs. Dubose dies.

◆ Mrs. Dubose was a morphine addict, determined to beat her addiction before she died.

◆ The reading sessions helped her to give up the pain-relieving morphine.

Atticus says Mrs. Dubose is *the bravest person I ever knew*. Mrs. Dubose's courage is seen in her determination to give up a drug that lessened her pain. Without realizing it, the children have helped her to fight and win her personal battle. Atticus wanted Jem and Scout to see this example of *real courage*. Atticus teaches the children the important lesson that there are different kinds of courage, and that Mrs. Dubose's bravery in enduring her pain so that she can face death with independence and self-respect is a truer example of courage than a man with a gun in his hand.

At the beginning of the chapter Jem and Scout see Mrs Dubose as an ill-natured old woman. In the end they understand the agony she was in, and that the unpleasant, frightening attacks she had were caused by her morphine addiction.

Test yourself

? You've covered the first part of the book. Well done! Take ten minutes to review what you have discovered about the characters and the ideas.

? First, add to your Mind Maps and your Timeline. When you have done that, identify these characters.
   • Who is *the meanest man God ever blew breath into*?
   • Who *never took anything they can't pay back*?
   • Who *has never done an honest day's work*?
   • Who pretended to plunge scissors into Dill's thigh?
   • Who wears an old straw hat and men's coveralls?
   • Who says, *I wanted you to see what true courage is*?

the trial beckons — take some time out before you go on

The second part of the novel focuses on the Tom Robinson trial. Some of the characters you have already met, such as the Ewells and the Cunninghams, have their part to play in this, and Boo Radley has an important role as well. Scout, Jem and Dill continue to grow up and to learn more about the society they live in and the people they live with.

Chapter 12

A visit to Calpurnia's church

(To *and we made our way homeward.*)

◆ Dill's mother remarries and he has to stay in Meridian for the summer.
◆ When Atticus is away, Calpurnia takes the children to her church.

Jem is growing up and changing. With the help of Atticus and Calpurnia, Scout begins to adjust to the changes in Jem. She misses Dill, but we see her child's view of life when she says she was miserable for two whole days! ✪ What do you feel about Dill's new situation?

Notice that the African-American community has its own church, known as First Purchase. The children's visit to it extends their education in a number of ways. ✪ How do the African-Americans greet the children? What does this tell you about the relationship between them and whites? Why doesn't Scout comment on this behavior? Lula objects to their presence because they are white. ✪ Does this tell you anything about the nature of prejudice? What do you think about Calpurnia's reply to Lula? Who does Calpurnia remind you of?

Scout is fascinated by how different this church and this service is from what she is used to. ✪ What does the custom of singing hymns by *lining* tell you about the community? What does the collection for Helen Robinson and the way it is gathered tell you about the community?

"A modest double life"

(From *"Cal, I know Tom Robinson's in jail,"* to end of chapter.)

◆ The children learn more about Calpurnia.
◆ Aunt Alexandra comes to stay.

Scout realizes two things about Calpurnia: that she is different from most of the other African-Americans, and that she leads two separate lives, one in her own home and community and one with the Finches. She can read, and had taught her son to read. She talks *"nigger talk"* with her own people because it would annoy them if she spoke in a *better* way. We see Scout's new awareness of Calpurnia as an individual when Scout asks if she can visit her home.

It's a shock when we see Aunt Alexandra waiting for them! ◐ Why has Aunt Alexandra come? How might her presence affect the children?

Over to you

? By now you will have gathered information about Tom Robinson and the forthcoming trial. You should know who is accusing him of what, and something about the effect on his family as well as on the Finch family. Put your ideas down in a Mind Map.

Chapter 13

Living with Aunt Alexandra

(From *"Put my bag in the front bedroom,"* to the end of the chapter.)

◆ Atticus explains that Aunt Alexandra will be staying for the summer.
◆ Aunt Alexandra tries to impose her own ideas on the family.
◆ Aunt Alexandra fits in well in Maycomb.

Aunt Alexandra is very concerned with correct behavior and with the importance of family background and the Finches' position as an old Maycomb family. Scout is irritated by her aunt's ideas that she should be more *feminine*, but does manage to hold her tongue. Jem is amused by the way Aunt Alexandra praises the Finches above all other local families. We see that Atticus disagrees with his sister about living up to the family name. He agrees to talk to the children about it but gives up.

On the other hand, the neighbors welcome Aunt Alexandra.
❂ Why does Aunt Alexandra fit in so well?

Try this

?   This chapter reinforces and adds to some of the ideas you have already gathered about life in Maycomb. Draw a Mind Map of Maycomb. Show what kind of town it is and what values it holds.

STYLE AND LANGUAGE

This chapter provides some light humor through its gentle, mocking tone. Family snobbery is ridiculed through expressions like *tribal groups* and the observation that Aunt Alexandra equates family worth with how long it has *been squatting on one patch of land*. We also have the amusing irony of Atticus trying to explain gentle breeding to Scout as she searches for a red bug on her leg.

take a break before Aunt Alexandra is even more annoying, and a runaway arrives

Chapter 14

"His maddening superiority"

(To *a phrase that united us again*.)

◆ Atticus and Aunt Alexandra disagree about Calpurnia.
◆ Scout fights Jem.

Notice how the tension gradually increases as the children hear anti-Finch comments in the town. Look at how Atticus answers when Scout asks what rape is. ○ How is his answer different from Uncle Jack's (Chapter 9)?

Aunt Alexandra disapproves of the children's visit to Calpurnia's church, and insists that Scout should not visit Calpurnia's home. She thinks Atticus should get rid of Calpurnia. ○ What are Aunt Alexandra's reasons for these views? What do you think of them? Atticus is strong in his support of Calpurnia. Can you think of examples to illustrate the points he makes in Calpurnia's favor?

Scout is upset by the quarrel between Atticus and Aunt Alexandra and is furious when Jem tells her not to antagonize their aunt. It's the last straw for Scout when Jem refers to himself as a grown-up, and she starts a fight by punching him. Atticus has to sort it out. ○ What different pressures is Atticus under? Who has a better understanding of them, Jem or Scout?

Something under the bed

(From *Ours were adjoining rooms*, to the end of the chapter.)

◆ Scout finds Dill hiding under the bed.
◆ Dill has run away from home because he feels unwanted.
◆ Jem tells Atticus that Dill is there.

Dill gives a highly colored account of his trip from Meridian before telling the true facts. Notice that he feels he is now *home*. ○ In what ways is the Finch household Dill's home? How is it different from his real home?

Jem breaks the remaining code of their childhood when he tells Atticus of Dill's presence. ○ Why does Jem do this? What else does Jem do and say in this chapter that shows that he is growing up and moving away from a child's point of view? Atticus is sensitive and tactful in the way he deals with Dill's arrival. His customary dry humor is reassuring.

Scout finds it hard to understand Dill's reason for leaving. Unlike Dill, she is secure in the love of her family and her place in it. Dill feels that his mother and stepfather don't want him around. ○ What do you think of Dill's account of life at home? There is pathos in the account of Dill crawling into Scout's bed and sharing his innocent fantasies. ❂ Why does Dill want to have a baby?

Your turn

? Take ten minutes to add to your Mind Maps of Atticus and of Dill. This is also a good time to show Jem's and Scout's progress up the Tree.

? Here is a good way of remembering some main characteristics of Dill:

> **D**reamy
> **I**maginative
> **L**onely
> **L**onging

the next chapter involves an ugly scene with a lynch mob. Take a short break first.

Chapter 15

The Saturday before the trial

(To *all he would say to my questions was go on and leave him alone.*)

◆ Dill is allowed to stay.

◆ Heck Tate, Link Deas, Dr. Reynolds, Mr. Avery, and other men visit Atticus.

◆ They think there will be trouble when Tom is brought to the local jail.

 The tension surrounding the trial builds up as the men warn Atticus that there may be trouble from the *Old Sarum bunch*, and question the wisdom of Atticus taking on the case. We can sense the ugliness in the racial tension and prejudice that threatens Tom's safety even before he comes to trial. Atticus doesn't waver and later reassures Jem that the men weren't out to harm him. Jem, however, is still concerned for Atticus's safety.

The Sunday before the trial

(From *Next day was Sunday*, to the end of the chapter.)

◆ Atticus sits outside the jail to guard Tom.
◆ The children follow him.
◆ A lynch mob led by Mr. Cunningham arrives at the jail.
◆ Scout unknowingly diffuses the situation by chatting to Mr. Cunningham.

This section is packed with drama. The children watch from the shadows of a shop door as the cars arrive and Atticus faces the men moving toward the jail. Atticus shows fear only when the children emerge from their hiding place. Jem refuses to go home. ❍ What do you think of Jem's behavior here? Notice Scout's limited understanding. She sees only an instance of Jem getting into trouble because he is defying Atticus.

Scout recognizes Mr. Cunningham and puts into practice what Atticus has taught her about social politeness. She tries to talk about a variety of subjects she thinks he might be interested in, including his son Walter and the nature of entailments. ❍ Does Scout understand the situation? Why do you think Mr. Cunningham leads the mob away?

As they walk home Dill carries the chair for Atticus. ❍ What does this gesture suggest? Once more we see Scout's childish perspective as she assumes that Jem is in trouble with Atticus for not going home. Atticus ruffles Jem's hair. ❍ What might this gesture mean?

Now try this

❔ You should have some interesting ideas to add to the Cunninghams on the Mind Map you started in Chapter 2. Take ten minutes to do this.

Chapter 16

The day of the trial

(To *and babies lunched at their mothers' breasts.*)

◆ Atticus discusses the lynch mob with his family.
◆ The children watch the townspeople going to the trial.
◆ In spite of being told not to, the children go to the courtroom.

We see that Atticus is beginning to make things clear to Aunt Alexandra when he disagrees with her. Here he says that Cal has his respect as one of the family and that he can speak frankly in front of her. Aunt Alexandra thinks there will be trouble if white people's prejudice is spoken of openly.

Atticus says that Scout's intervention the night before reminded Mr. Cunningham that he was a person, not just a member of a mob. Atticus believes that human beings are basically good. ✪ What lesson or belief does Atticus refer to when he explains what Scout achieved? At first, Mr. Cunningham saw Atticus as the person wrongly protecting Tom Robinson. ✪ How do you think he saw Atticus after Scout's conversation?

Crowds of spectators flock to the courtroom. ✪ How would you describe the atmosphere? Why do people want to see a trial that will have a predictable outcome? Do the whites and the blacks have different expectations? Why does Miss Maudie choose not to go?

The trial begins

(From *In a far corner of the square*, to the end of the chapter.)

◆ The children discuss Mr. Dolphus Raymond.
◆ Reverend Sykes helps the children get seats on the "Colored" balcony.

Jem explains that Dolphus Raymond seems to prefer the company of African-Americans. He lives with a African-American woman and has several bi-racial children, whom he treats well. He is known to be a drunk. ✪ Are you surprised that

Dolphus Raymond is not part of the Maycomb community? What do you think about the situation of his children?

Scout overhears a spectator say that Atticus was appointed to defend Tom Robinson. She wonders why Atticus has never used this fact as an excuse. ✪ How does this knowledge confirm your opinion of Atticus?

The blacks are divided from the whites in court, another example of how physical divisions reflect deeper inequalities. ✪ What does the sight of the children sitting in the "Colored" balcony suggest about their sympathies? Can you think of anyone else in Maycomb who would want to sit there, or be welcome there?

Judge Taylor has some eccentric habits. ✪ Can you find some examples? Is he thought to be a good judge?

Over to you

? Here are some of the people present at the trial. Decide which ones have a good reason for going to court. Give each a mark out of ten to show how far you support their presence at the trial. Stephanie Crawford, Dolphus Raymond, the Mennonites (a strict Christian sect), Heck Tate, the "Idlers' Club," Reverend Sykes, Scout, Jem, Dill.

? Remember to add to your Timeline.

Chapters 17-21 describe the trial in detail, but take a quick break first

Heck Tate's testimony

Chapter 17

(To *and stepped down from the witness stand.*)

◆ The sheriff reports that he was called to the Ewell house in November on a rape accusation.

- ◆ He found Mayella Ewell with injuries on the right side of her face and round her neck.
- ◆ The sheriff arrested Tom Robinson following Mayella's identification.
- ◆ No doctor was called.

Atticus highlights two important issues: the position of Mayella's injuries, and the fact that no one called a doctor. ✪ Why should a doctor have been summoned? Jem recognizes the significance of the fact that a doctor wasn't called, but Scout doesn't. ✪ Why is the position of the injuries important? Is the right or the left hand likely to inflict bruises on the right side of someone's face?

Bob Ewell takes the witness stand

(From *Below us, heads turned*, to *past the Ewell residence*.)

- ◆ Mr. Ewell takes the oath.
- ◆ Scout describes the Ewells.

Bob Ewell's physical appearance and manner reflect his cocky, aggressive personality. We hear more about the Ewell way of life and their home behind the town garbage dump. Their cabin looks like the playhouse of an insane child with its ramshackle collection of broken and rusty implements and rubbish. Look at the comparison with the neat and snug cabins in the African-American settlement. ✪ How does knowledge of his poverty and deprivation affect your attitude to Bob Ewell?

Try this

? In contrast to the rest of the home, there are six geraniums in a corner of the yard. What do the flowers suggest about the person who tends them?

? What qualities do you associate with flowers?

? Write a word in each of the flower jars on next page.

Bob Ewell's evidence

(From *All the little man on the witness stand*, to the end of the chapter.)

- ◆ Bob Ewell says he saw the rape taking place.
- ◆ Atticus establishes once more that a doctor wasn't called.
- ◆ Atticus establishes that Bob Ewell is left-handed.

The way in which Bob Ewell gives his evidence reveals his prejudice, ignorance, and coarseness. Judge Taylor reprimands him for his attitude and crude language and the African-Americans in court are angered by his inflammatory words. He refers to the African-American settlement as a *nigger-nest*. ✪ How would you describe the tone of this phrase and the attitude it shows? How are the houses of the African-American community different from the Ewell house? What does this tell you about Bob?

Ewell doesn't understand the purpose of Atticus's questions. He doesn't see that his failure to get medical attention for his daughter hints at lack of concern and possibly guilt and that the fact that he is left-handed suggests that he could have caused the injuries on the right side of Mayella's face. However, Ewell entertains the crowd with his smart answers, then accuses Atticus of trickery. ✪ How do you think the jury will react to Ewell's performance on the witness stand?

55

Now try this

? Make a Mind Map to help you to track the progress of the trial. You could use the one that has been started here, or you could start your own. Spend about ten minutes on it.

*C*hapter 18

"You makin' fun o' me?"

(To "*He never touched me.*")

◆ Mayella says that Tom Robinson did a job for her, then hit her and raped her.

◆ Atticus's questions reveal a picture of Mayella's life.

Mayella is frightened and tearful as she gives her evidence. When Atticus speaks to her with his usual politeness, she thinks he is mocking her, and she thinks he is making fun of her when he asks about her friends.

Gently Atticus builds up a picture of Mayella's impoverished, deprived life. We see the struggle to keep clean and clothed, the constant hunger and illnesses, the lack of education, and the lack of love. ○ What do you think about Mayella's way of life? Mayella won't admit that her father hits her. ○ Do you think she is telling the truth? Why might she lie?

Mayella's evidence

(From *Atticus's glasses had slipped a little*, to the end of the chapter.)

◆ Atticus gets Mayella to repeat her story of what happened.
◆ Tom Robinson rises to be identified, and his withered left arm is revealed.
◆ Mayella sticks to her story.
◆ She gets angry when Atticus continues to question her.

 There is great tension in the moment when Tom rises to his feet. Notice the way that Harper Lee creates dramatic effect by revealing his damaged arm only at this moment. Scout and Jem realize that Tom could not have used his left hand to hit Mayella. Mayella blusters through a repeated account of what happened. She is silent when asked where the other children were and is silent when Atticus suggests that her father was the one who beat her up.

Atticus feels compassion for Mayella. ☉ Does Mayella realize this? Why does she look with hatred at Atticus?

Over to you

? You have heard the case for the prosecution. Write on the illustration below any evidence or circumstances against Tom Robinson. If you need to you can add weights and fill in more points.

Chapter 19

"I felt right sorry for her"

(From *Thomas Robinson reached around*, to the end of the chapter.)

◆ Tom states that he had done jobs for Mayella a number of times.

◆ On this occasion Mayella invited him into the house and made advances to him.

◆ Tom tried to escape.

◆ He ran away when Mr. Ewell arrived.

◆ Dill cries during the cross-examination of Tom, and Scout takes him outside.

Look at the way Tom's left hand slips off the Bible as he takes the oath. ❂ What idea does this confirm? Tom's answers to Atticus's questions are clear and straightforward, and give a different version from Mayella's story. ❂ Who does Scout believe? At what points does Tom become uncomfortable and nervous?

Tom's good nature, kindness, and sensitivity are apparent in the way he treated Mayella and in the way he talks about her now. ❂ Which of the white characters have these qualities? The court responds at two main points: when Tom says Mayella hugged him, and when he says he felt sorry for her. Tom cannot win. A black person who presumes to show sympathy for a white is thought to be insulting and impertinent.

Notice the different reactions of Dill and Scout. Scout is used to the practice of cross-examination and knows the prosecuting lawyer is expected to act in a harsh way. ❂ Does Atticus ever put on an act? She also says Tom is *just a Negro*. Dill's response is more raw and emotional. Unlike Scout, he is not conditioned by the traditions and conventions of Maycomb, and his humanity is outraged by what is happening.

Your turn

? Fill in the other side of the scales illustration on p. 57.
with all the facts or circumstances on Tom's side.

? Add as many weights as you need to.

? Add to your Mind Map of the trial.

Chapter 20

The simple hell people give others

(To *"Hush now."*)

◆ Dolphus Raymond gives Dill a Coca-Cola to settle his
stomach.

◆ He tells Dill and Scout that he just pretends to be a heavy
drinker.

Dolphus Raymond explains to the children that he lets
people think he is a drunkard so that they can excuse his
unacceptable behavior. The people of Maycomb need to
think that he can't change his way of life, and are unable
to understand that he doesn't want to. From their point of
view, no normal person would live in racial harmony as he
does. ○ What do you think about Dolphus Raymond's way of
coping with prejudice? Notice that he speaks highly of Atticus.
○ What does he have in common with Atticus? How is he
different from Atticus?

Dolphus Raymond has experienced the hell white
people give *colored folks*. He recognizes that Dill is
seeing it for the first time, and that is why Dill is crying. He
says that it won't affect Dill so much when he gets a bit older.
○ What do you think about the idea that people become
hardened and learn to live with things they know are wrong?

"In the name of God, believe him."

(From *We looked down again*, to the end of the chapter.)

- ◆ Atticus sums up his case for the jury.
- ◆ He explains that Mayella made advances to Tom.
- ◆ Bob Ewell saw this through the window.
- ◆ He beat Mayella for her behavior.
- ◆ Mayella said that Tom had raped her.
- ◆ Atticus begs the jury to set aside prejudice and declare Tom innocent.

Atticus's speech reflects the heart of the novel. He presents the evidence for Tom's innocence clearly and eloquently. He makes the jury face their prejudice, the deep, ingrained, evil assumption that all African-Americans are untrustworthy and that a white person's word should always be accepted over theirs. Atticus asks the jury to question their false assumptions and to give Tom equal standing in the eyes of the law, as is his right as a human being. Atticus speaks with the humanity, compassion, integrity, and passionate concern for justice that define his character.

STYLE AND LANGUAGE

Atticus's style of address is clear and elegant. Notice that he doesn't use highly-colored language or emotive words to sway the jury, nor does he over-simplify the issues at stake. The language he uses and the tone of his speech indicate respect for the jury's intelligence and confidence in their ability to understand the arguments he presents. He uses comparisons to make his points clear, as when he says Mayella is like a child trying to hide stolen goods. The stinging sarcasm in the description of Bob Ewell as a *God-fearing, persevering, respectable white man* shows Atticus's contempt for Ewell's cynical behavior. His tone here is a contrast to the conversational way he begins his speech and the intensity he builds up to at the end.

The reference to Thomas Jefferson's Declaration of Independence gives Atticus's argument a universal application, and the passion of Atticus's belief in justice and equality can be felt in the rhythm of his rhetoric as he balances phrases: *the pauper the equal of a Rockefeller, the stupid man the equal of an Einstein.*

Over to you

?   Add Atticus's speech to your Mind Map of the trial.

treat yourself to a break before the jury deliver their verdict

Chapter 21

Waiting for the verdict

(To *and I was too weary to argue.*)

◆ Calpurnia arrives and takes the children home.
◆ They get permission to return to hear the verdict.
◆ Jem is convinced that Atticus has won.

Calpurnia and Aunt Alexandra are aghast that the children witnessed the trial. ✪ Does Scout understand why the adults think the trial was unsuitable for them? Reverend Sykes says that Judge Taylor's final address to the jury was fair, perhaps leaning a little to Tom's side. ✪ What do you think of the way Judge Taylor conducted the trial? Has he been fair? Has he kept order?

Jem is exultant. He thinks the case Atticus presented is so convincing that no jury could convict Tom. He overrides Reverend Sykes's warning that he has never known a jury to favor a black man over a white. ✪ What are your feelings for Jem at this point?

Guilty

(From *But I must have been reasonably awake,* to the end of the chapter.)

◆ The jury gives its verdict.
◆ They find Tom Robinson guilty.

The atmosphere in court reminds Scout of the morning when Atticus shot the dog. There is the same tense stillness and the same sense of movement as slow and dreamlike as if underwater. On that occasion the mockingbirds were quiet. ✷ What does this suggest about the coming verdict? Think about the kind of courage that was shown on that occasion. ✷ What kind of courage will be needed now? Who will need to be brave?

Atticus has lost the case, but the African-American spectators stand up as he passes. ✷ Why do they do this?

Your turn

? You can now complete your Mind Map of the trial.

Chapter 22

The aftermath

(To *Makes you feel like you've done something*.)

◆ Atticus says he will appeal the verdict.
◆ The African-Americans send gifts of food to Atticus.

Jem is filled with anger and bitterness at the verdict. He can't understand or accept such injustice. Atticus doesn't try to make make it better, but says that the kind of prejudice the children have witnessed is a part of Maycomb and they will have to learn to cope with it. ✷ Do you agree with Atticus that *only children weep* over this kind of injustice? Atticus is moved to tears by the African-American community's generosity in sending food in such hard times.

Scout notices, but doesn't understand Aunt Alexandra calling Atticus *brother*. ✷ What is Aunt Alexandra feeling? Are the children the only ones who "grow" in the course of the novel?

"It's just a baby-step, but it's a step"

(From *Miss Maudie yelled for Jem Finch*, to the end of the chapter.)

◆ Miss Maudie discusses the trial with the children.
◆ Bob Ewell spits at Atticus and threatens revenge.

Miss Maudie shows her distaste for Stephanie Crawford's pleasure in gossiping about the trial. ☉ Why has Miss Maudie not made a little cake for Jem? We see her sensitivity and understanding as she explains that Atticus has the courage to put into practice his Christian beliefs about equality. By defending Tom, Atticus was acting on behalf of all the people in the town who are on the side of justice. Miss Maudie comforts Jem by pointing out that Atticus made the jury think. It took them a long time to come to their decision. ☉ What was Miss Maudie thinking as she waited for the verdict? Why did Judge Taylor choose Atticus to take the case? Can you remember any other time when Miss Maudie helped the children to understand Atticus?

We see Dill's despair and disillusion as he declares he will be a new kind of clown and laugh at other people. He can't respect his God-fearing Aunt Rachel, with her dismissive attitude to Atticus and her morning drinking. Dill sees nothing to admire in the behavior of the majority of adults in his life.

Over to you

❓ Put together all your ideas about Miss Maudie. Think about the kind of person she is and what she contributes to the book's themes and ideas.

more about the trial and its effects after the break

Chapter 23

"Stand in Bob Ewell's shoes"

(To *Jem muttered*.)

◆ Atticus is not alarmed by Bob Ewell's assault.
◆ Atticus and Jem discuss the legal system.

Atticus reacts calmly to Bob Ewell's threats, although the children and Aunt Alexandra fear for his safety. Atticus's urging them to see the trial from Bob's point of view shows the consistency of his principles and his continued humanity. He would rather Bob take his anger out on him than on the Ewell children. ✪ Why does Ewell want revenge even though he got the verdict he wanted? Do you think Atticus is right not to worry about what Bob Ewell might do? Could Aunt Alexandra be right for once?

Jem's views on capital offenses, the nature of evidence and the jury system show his understanding and his intelligence. Atticus makes him face the fact that juries are not guided by reason when it is a white man's word against a black man's. Prejudice and resentment make otherwise reasonable men behave irrationally and unfairly. We see how strongly Atticus feels when he says that a white man who cheats a black man is *trash*. ✪ Why is Atticus pleased when Jem asks about how juries are made up? What do you feel about their jokes about women serving on juries?

One member of the jury

(From *Atticus's fingers went to his watch-pocket,* to the end of the chapter.)

◆ Atticus reveals that Mr. Cunningham wanted Tom to be acquitted.
◆ Aunt Alexandra insists that Finches should not associate with Cunninghams.
◆ Jem tells Scout about the different kinds of people in the world.

Mr. Cunningham was responsible for the *baby-step* of making the jury stay out for a few hours. We see Atticus's shrewd instinct in his decision to have Mr. Cunningham on the jury, even though he had threatened Tom and Atticus the night outside the jail. Atticus felt that Mr. Cunningham had increased respect for the Finches after that incident. ✪ We see one man leaning forward with hands over the railing as Bob Ewell signs his name in the court. Who might that man be? Why is he leaning forward?

Notice the difference between Scout's spontaneous, innocent response that she would like to be friends with Walter Cunningham now, and Aunt Alexandra's adherence to family and class divisions. ✪ Compare Aunt Alexandra's use of the word *trash* with Atticus's earlier use. What is the difference in the way they judge people? Jem explains his way of classifying people in Maycomb county into four groups. Notice the way he attempts to understand the social and racial differences between the family groups, unlike Scout, who thinks there are just people. ✪ What do you think?

We see Jem's increased understanding of Boo Radley when he says Boo wants to stay inside. His comment also reflects Jem's growing awareness of the harsh reality of the world. Jem is growing up physically and emotionally. ✪ How is he like Atticus? How is he different from him?

Test yourself

?   How much have you learned about the different families and groups in Maycomb? Fill in the gaps.

The_____ are known to be stubborn.

The_____ believe that pleasure is a sin.

The_____ live out in the woods.

The_____ live by the dump.

The_____ have got *background* and *good breeding*.

The_____ children *don't belong anywhere*.

*C*hapter 24

The ladies of Maycomb

(To *when he doesn't know for sure it's so*.)

◆ Scout attends a missionary tea.

 Scout dresses in appropriate "feminine" clothes for the occasion, and helps Calpurnia by carrying in the coffee.

❂ Has Scout changed? What has she learned? Notice the way Miss Maudie silently supports Scout and helps her to endure Stephanie Crawford's spiteful teasing about the children's presence at the trial.

Grace Merriweather tells the missionary circle about the plight of a poor African tribe and a *saintly* white missionary who works with them. There is strong irony in the fact that the ladies have no regard for the African-Americans in their own community, and are highly critical of the white lawyer who acts on their behalf. They think that Atticus just caused trouble by defending Tom. ❂ Are the ladies hypocritical? Do they recognize the contradictions in their attitudes?

The ladies are aware of the unrest among the African-American population following Tom's trial. They call this response unchristian, and find it unpleasant to deal with sulky, dissatisfied people. ❂ How do the ladies think the African-American community should react?

Miss Maudie shows her anger at the criticism of Atticus, and Aunt Alexandra is grateful for her support. This is another example of how Aunt Alexandra has come to understand the great strain that taking on the Robinson case has imposed on Atticus. ❂ Does this mean that Aunt Alexandra now thinks he was right to take on the case?

"Tom's dead"

(from *The front door slammed*, to the end of the chapter.)

◆ Atticus arrives with the news that Tom Robinson is dead.
◆ Tom was shot while trying to escape from prison.
◆ Atticus and Cal go to break the news to Helen, Tom's wife.
◆ Aunt Alexandra hides her strong feelings and continues her role as hostess.
◆ Scout follows her example.

Tom's desperate break for freedom highlights the despair and isolation we imagine him feeling. ❂ Why didn't he wait for the appeal? What does Atticus think about the number of bullet holes in Tom? Why was Tom shot so often?

Notice Aunt Alexandra's concern for her brother. She acknowledges his moral courage and hates the way he is being torn to pieces by the demands it places on him. Once again Miss Maudie interprets Atticus's position, saying that he acts on behalf of the handful of people in Maycomb who share his views on justice and equality. ❖ Name as many of these people as you can. Miss Maudie says these people have *background*. ❖ How is her use of the word different from Aunt Alexandra's, and from Jem's in Chapter 23?

Scout follows Aunt Alexandra's example and continues to offer hospitality. She now sees that the ability to control one's feelings and to behave courteously in public are an important part of being a lady. Scout accepts that she has to enter the world of Maycomb ladies, but knows that she will find it difficult. Scout is uneasy with its conventions and prefers the directness and honesty of her father's world. ❖ What do you like/admire about the ideas of "ladies" behavior shown in the book? ❖ What do you dislike?

Your turn

? In this chapter the Maycomb ladies present their view of the African-American community. What do you think about the way the African-Americans are shown? Focus on the main characters: Cal, Tom, and Reverend Sykes. Are there any African-American characters who are immoral or untrustworthy? Is the African-American community idealized?

? Show your ideas in a Mind Map.

STYLE AND LANGUAGE

The reference to mockingbirds in this chapter focuses our attention on Tom Robinson as the central "mockingbird" figure. Tom is presented as an innocent, good character. Not only does he not do any harm, but he displays positive qualities of kindness, compassion, and generosity. Just as the mockingbird sings its heart out naturally, so Tom's life and actions are a natural, spontaneous expression of his humanity and decency. Just as the mockingbird is slaughtered by thoughtless people, so Tom is slaughtered. ❖ Who kills Tom? Are the prison guards who shoot him the only ones responsible?

you'll see the effects of Tom's death in the next chapter, but first take a break

Chapter 25

Killing a mockingbird

(From *"Don't do that, Scout,"* to the end of the chapter.)

◆ Dill and Jem go with Atticus to tell Tom's wife of his death.
◆ Maycomb doesn't show any sympathy for Tom.
◆ Mr. Underwood writes about Tom's death in The Maycomb Tribune.
◆ Bob Ewell continues his threats.

Scout is irritated when Jem tells her not to squash an insect she is playing with because it hasn't done her any harm. Dill reports that when Helen Robinson heard that her husband was dead, she collapsed as if a giant with a big foot had stepped on her. ✪ Can you see a connection between these incidents? How do they fit in with the book's themes and ideas?

Maycomb interprets Tom's attempt to escape as being *typical* of an African-American's irrational behavior. Tom's action confirms the townspeople's prejudices and gives them an opportunity to dismiss his life and his death as insignificant. Mr. Underwood, however, is bitterly critical of Tom's killing, and likens his death to *the senseless slaughter of songbirds*. Mr. Underwood's editorial helps Scout to realize the limitations of the law. In spite of the legal system, the weight of evidence, the jury, and the defense, Tom Robinson could never be found innocent. In *the secret court of men's hearts* he was guilty from the moment he was accused.

Over to you

? Each of the items on p. 69 has appeared in the story. Use each illustration as the center of a Mind Map to show its importance in the book.

Chapter 26

Pre-ju-dice

(From *School started*, to the end of the chapter.)

◆ Scout's attitude to Boo Radley has changed.
◆ In a Current Events class Miss Gates discusses Hitler's treatment of the Jews.
◆ Jem is disturbed by the memory of the courtroom.

We see how much Scout has grown up in the way she now feels *a twinge of remorse* for the way they used to bother Boo Radley. She is still fascinated by him, though. Notice how she fantasizes about meeting him and exchanging normal, conventional greetings as if they met every day.

In class, Miss Gates speaks with pride of the lack of prejudice in America, and condemns the *terrible* persecution of the Jews since the beginning of history. Scout can't understand how Miss Gates can speak out passionately against Hitler yet support the treatment of the African-Americans in her own town. ❂ Where else has Scout heard sympathy expressed for blacks in other countries? What does this teach Scout about people and their beliefs? What do you think is the author's opinion of Miss Gates?

Scout's reference to the conversation outside the courtroom hits a raw nerve with Jem. ✪ Why does Jem want to forget about the trial? Why do you think he wants to be a football player?

Try this

? This chapter adds to the contrast we see throughout the book in the way of life of the poor rural community (like the Cunninghams) and the people who live in the town (like the Finches). Use the illustrations to help you to jot down some ideas about the differences between them.

T O W N | C O U N T R Y

Chapter 27

Three threats

(To *Atticus chuckled.*)

◆ Bob Ewell thinks Atticus cost him his job.
◆ Judge Taylor has an intruder in his house.

◆ Bob Ewell follows Helen Robinson to work.

Bob Ewell's behavior shows that he still bears a grudge against those involved in the trial. We see his cowardice in the way he complains behind Atticus's back, tries to break into Judge Taylor's house when he thinks it's empty, and harasses and verbally assaults Helen, who is vulnerable because she is African-American. Atticus understands that Ewell feels resentful because although he won the case, he looked foolish and didn't gain the respect he thought he would. Atticus thinks these actions will have eased Ewell's feelings. ✪ What do you think?

Chicken wire and brown cloth

(From *By the end of October*, to the end of the chapter.)

◆ A community celebration of Halloween is planned, including a pageant.
◆ Scout is to represent "Pork" as an example of Maycomb's agricultural produce.
◆ Scout has to wear a costume making her look like a cured ham.

We are reminded of the economic situation when Atticus explains to Scout that the National Recovery Act, which was part of President Roosevelt's plan to help the country out of the Depression, has been cancelled.

The amusing way the pageant and Scout's costume in particular are presented provides a contrast to the forthcoming crisis. The light-hearted joke played on Miss Tutti and Miss Frutti emphasizes the seriousness of what is to come. Scout's innocent delight in her costume heightens our awareness of the crucial role the costume plays later. ✪ What do you think Atticus and Aunt Alexandra think of Scout's role and her costume? Do you think they want to go to the pageant? Tension mounts as we sense Aunt Alexandra's feeling that something is wrong. As Scout and Jem set out alone on their longest journey together, we are prepared for danger to come.

Your turn

?   Look back at the Prejudice Scale you did at the end of
Chapter 5. Decide where the following characters fit
in and add them to your list. You might want to
change some of your original ideas.

Judge Taylor, Link Deas, Dolphus Raymond,
Mr. Underwood, Mrs. Merriweather.

*treat yourself to a short break and prepare
for a brutal attack*

Chapter 28

Scout the star

(To *Let's go*.)

◆ Jem and Scout walk to the school in the dark.
◆ Cecil Jacobs jumps out at them.
◆ Scout falls asleep and misses her cue.
◆ Scout keeps her costume on.
◆ Scout and Jem wait until the audience has left, then set out
for home.

The atmosphere is eerie and foreboding as the children
walk through the dark past the Radley place. The
reference to the mockingbird adds a poignant touch,
reminding us both of the solitary, innocent Boo inside the
house and the ugliness of the evil we will soon encounter.
Scout and Jem laugh at their younger selves who believed in
magic and spirits, but they are still frightened when Cecil leaps
out at them. This mock attack foreshadows the real attack that
will follow.

Scout is humiliated when she is scolded for wandering onto
the stage at the wrong time and ruining the pageant. We see
Jem's growing tact and sensitivity as he reassures Scout and
shows he understands how she is feeling.

"Run, Scout!"

(From *We went through the auditorium*, to *I smelled stale whisky*.)

◆ Jem and Scout hear someone following them.
◆ Someone attacks Scout and Jem.
◆ An unknown man pulls Scout's attacker off her.
◆ Scout finds a man's body on the ground.

We feel the tension as Jem thinks he hears someone following them and the children try to convince themselves it's just their imagination, or Cecil. Scout's sudden calling out to startle Cecil rings emptily and eerily in the darkness. Notice how the children, unable to see in the dark, are aware of sounds – rustling, dragging, shuffling – that tell them they are being followed. The suddenness of the attack is effectively conveyed through the short sentences, and Scout's confusion can be felt in her impressions of scuffling, kicking, scraping, ripping.

❍ Does the attacker expect Scout to be enclosed in chicken wire? What might have happened if she hadn't been wearing her costume? Scout thinks that the man who saved them might be Atticus, but he walks away toward the road. ❍ What is Scout thinking as she tries to identify the body on the ground? Are we given clues about his identity?

Bob Ewell is dead

(From *I made my way along*, to the end of the chapter.)

◆ The man who saved them is carrying Jem home.
◆ Dr. Reynolds and Heck Tate are called.
◆ Jem has a broken arm.
◆ Heck Tate says that Bob Ewell is lying dead with a kitchen knife in him.

We see Atticus's and Aunt Alexandra's panic and concern. Notice the gentleness and sympathy with which Aunt Alexandra unwinds the wire and fabric from Scout. She is so concerned and distracted that she gives Scout her overalls to put on, garments she hates to see Scout wear.

Remind yourself of the very first sentence in the book. Here is a good example of the careful structure and patterning of the novel. ✪ Who else has a damaged left arm? What is the connection between Bob Ewell and these two injuries?

Scout's greatest concern is that Jem is dead, and she shows little curiosity about the man who brought Jem home. The chapter ends dramatically with the news of Ewell's death and the unexplained mystery about the man in the corner.

Over to you

? The Ewells have lost their father. Think about the kind of parent Bob was, and about other parents you have met in the novel, such as Atticus and Dill's parents. Do any characters have the function of parents? Make a Mind Map to show your thoughts about different kinds of parents and the qualities they show.

Chapter 29

"Hey, Boo"

(From *Aunt Alexandra got up*, to the end of the chapter.)

◆ Scout tells Heck Tate what happened.
◆ Scout realizes that the man who saved them was Boo Radley.

We see Atticus and Aunt Alexandra under great strain. Aunt Alexandra blames herself for not acting on the feeling she had that something was going to happen, and Atticus never imagined that Bob Ewell would attack his children. ✪ How is Atticus's view of people different from Heck Tate's? Which do you agree with more?

Scout's account reflects the speed and confusion of the attack. Look at her broken sentences and her use of phrases like *somethin' grabbed me; sounded like; I reckon; I guess.*

Scout has her first view of Boo Radley. The first thing she notices is how white his skin is. ✪ Why is Boo so pale? Boo's body language shows how uncomfortable he is to be out of his own house. His arms are folded across his chest and his expression is tense. His tension goes as he smiles at Scout.

✪ Why is Scout tearful as she says "hello" to Boo?

Test yourself

?   The physical description of Boo Radley shows his frailty and lack of vitality. From the descriptions given, can you identify the characters below?

Someone who has a cowlick in the middle of his forehead.
Someone who looks and smells like a peppermint drop.
Someone who wears a clean shirt and neatly mended overalls.
Someone who wears an old straw hat and men's overalls.
Someone who is nearly blind in his left eye.
Someone who has old-age liver spots and knobbly hands.
Someone who chews cigars.
Someone who looks as if she tries to keep clean.

?   Remember to add to your Timeline.

time for a break before Atticus makes a mistake, and sticks to his principles

Chapter 30

"Bob Ewell fell on his knife"

(From "Mr. Arthur, honey," to the end of the chapter.)

◆ Atticus thinks that Jem killed Bob Ewell.
◆ Heck Tate explains that Boo Radley killed Ewell.
◆ Heck wants to keep this quiet, to protect Boo from the attention he would receive.
◆ Atticus agrees to stick to the story that Ewell died when he fell on his knife.

Scout is now aware of Boo as a human being with his own needs. She notices the matter-of-fact way Dr. Reynolds greets him, and understands when Atticus moves them to the porch away from the strong living room lights. Scout speaks to Boo in a friendly and courteous way, as if he were an ordinary visitor. She shows tact as she leads him to the rocking chair. ❂ Where else has Scout acted "like a lady" in very strange circumstances? Would the Scout we met at the beginning of the book have behaved like his?

Atticus insists that Jem should face the consequences of what Atticus believes he has done. Hushing it up would be a denial of how Atticus has brought up his children. If he bends the course of justice in this case, Atticus will lose his self-respect and his children's respect. ❂ What do you think about Atticus's position here? Can you see a similarity with the reasons he gave for defending Tom Robinson?

Heck Tate stands up to Atticus and insists on taking responsibility for his decision. Strictly speaking, Boo Radley's role in the evening's events and in Ewell's death should be made public. The Sheriff's words that it would be a sin to put Boo through such an ordeal remind us of the mockingbird symbol and the concern for humanity that is at the center of the novel. Heck is similar to Atticus here: they both respect the law and uphold the legal system, and at the same time they recognize that sometimes the law of humanity is more important. ❂ Can you think of another example from earlier in the book where we see the law being bent to protect the innocent?

Atticus need to know that Scout understands the reason for Ewell's death being described as an accident. Scout's reply shows how much she has come to understand Atticus's humanitarian principles and the shy, innocent nature of Boo Radley.

Your turn

? In this chapter we see Atticus facing another difficult decision. Think about the way he deals with it, then complete your Mind Map of Atticus.

Chapter 31

Standing in Boo's shoes

(From *When Boo Radley shuffled to his feet*, to the end of the chapter.)

◆ Scout takes Boo home.
◆ Scout stands on the Radley porch and surveys the neighborhood.
◆ Scout sees the events of the last two years from Boo's point of view.

Notice how Scout is sensitive to Boo's expressions and gestures. She knows Boo wants to touch Jem, and she knows when Boo wants to leave. We see her tact and understanding as she makes it seem as if Arthur is escorting her home, and not the other way around.

Scout puts herself in Boo's shoes. She sees Boo watching his children through all the seasons, from their early games with Dill until the moment of danger,when he finally came out to save their lives. Scout feels sad that they gave Boo nothing in return for his gifts. ○ Do you think they gave him anything?

Atticus's last words to Scout in the novel are that most people are nice when you finally see them. His faith in humanity is strong. We see him caring for Jem and Scout throughout this most difficult of evenings, and the novel ends with Scout's faith in his sympathy and consistency, qualities that she finally understands.

And finally

? Finish working on the Tree. If you like, you could take the ideas from there and present them in Mind Maps of Jem and Scout.

? Choose as many of the following words as you think describe the book, or part of it. Decide which references you would use to support your choice.

funny sad depressing exciting optimistic idealistic thought-provoking annoying painful well-structured

you've worked hard on the novel — well done! Take a well-earned break

TOPICS FOR DISCUSSION AND BRAINSTORMING

One of the best ways to review is with one or more friends. Even if you're with someone who hardly knows the text you're studying, you'll find that having to explain things to your friend will help you to organize your own thoughts and memorize key points. If you're with someone who has studied the text, you'll find that the things you can't remember are different from the things your friend can't remember, so you'll be able to help each other.

Discussion will also help you to develop interesting new ideas that perhaps neither of you would have had alone. Use a brainstorming approach to tackle any of the topics listed below. Allow yourself to share whatever ideas come into your head, however meaningless they seem. This will get you thinking creatively.

Whether alone or with a friend, use Mind Mapping (see p. vi) to help you brainstorm and organize your ideas. If you are with a friend, use a large sheet of paper and colored pens of different thickness.

Any of the topics below could appear on an exam, but even if you think you've found one in your actual exam, be sure to answer the precise question given.

TOPICS

1 Which two characters gain your sympathy most? Explain the reasons for your choice.
2 Atticus is criticized for the way he brings up his children. Do you think this criticism is fair?
3 What impression of life in Maycomb do you get from reading the book?
4 What do you find interesting about the relationship between Jem and Scout and how it develops?
5 What do you think is the most dramatic incident in the book, and what do you think is saddest? Write about each incident and show how its effect is created.

HOW TO GET AN "A" IN ENGLISH LITERATURE

In all your study, in coursework, and in exams, be aware of the following:

- **Characterization** – the characters and how we know about them (what they say and do, how the author describes them), their relationships, and how they develop.
- **Plot and structure** – what happens and how the plot is organized into parts or episodes.
- **Setting and atmosphere** – the changing scene and how it reflects the story (for example, the description of the Radley house suggesting coldness and isolation; the tense atmosphere in the courtroom).
- **Style and language** – the author's choice of words, and literary devices such as imagery, and how these reflect the mood.
- **Viewpoint** – how the story is told (for example, through an imaginary narrator, or in the third person but through the eyes of one character).
- **Social and historical context** – influences on the author (see Background in this guide).

Develop your ability to:

- Relate **detail** to **broader content, meaning, and style**.
- Show understanding of the author's **intentions, technique, and meaning** (brief and appropriate comparisons with other works by the same author will earn credit).
- Give **personal response and interpretation**, backed up by **examples** and short **quotations**.
- **Evaluate** the author's achievement (how far does the author succeed and why?)

Make sure you:

- Know how to use **paragraphs** correctly.
- Use a wide range of **vocabulary** and sentence structure.
- Use short appropriate quotations as **evidence** of your understanding of that part of the text.
- Use **literary terms** to show your understanding of what the author is trying to achieve with language.

THE EXAM ESSAY

Planning

A literary essay of about 250 to 400 words on a theme from *To Kill a Mockingbird* will challenge your skills as an essay writer. It is worth taking some time to plan your essay carefully. An excellent way to do this is in the three stages below:

1 Make a **Mind Map of** your ideas on the theme suggested. Brainstorm and write down any ideas that pop into your head.
2 Taking ideas from your Mind Map, **organize** them into an outline choosing a logical sequence of information. Choose significant details and quotations to support your main thesis.
3 Be sure you have both a strong **opening paragraph** stating your main idea and giving the title and author of the literary work you will be discussing, and a **conclusion** that sums up your main points.

Writing and Editing

Write your essay carefully, allowing at least five minutes at the end to check for errors of fact as well as for correct spelling, grammar, and punctuation.

REMEMBER!

Stick to the thesis you are trying to support and avoid unnecessary plot summary. Always support your ideas with relevant details and quotations from the text.

Model Answer and Plan

The next (and final) chapter consists of a model essay on a theme from *To Kill a Mockingbird* followed by a Mind Map and an essay plan used to write it. Use these to get an idea of how an essay about *To Kill a Mockingbird* might be organized and how to break up your information into a logical sequence of paragraphs.

Before reading the answer, you might like to do a plan of your own, then compare it with the example. The numbered points with comments at the end, show why it's a good answer.

MODEL ANSWER AND ESSAY PLAN

QUESTION

What do you think about the presentation of the African-American characters in *To Kill a Mockingbird*?

PLAN

1 Good – too good?
2 Contrast to white community.
3 Behavior at trial.
4 Environment – home, church.
5 Main characters.
6 Conclusion.

The African-American characters in *To Kill a Mockingbird* are shown in a very favorable light. Harper Lee wants to make us aware of the injustice and prejudice that African-Americans suffer, and in her wish to make us admire the African-American community, makes them appear a little too good to be true.

In many ways she presents them as superior to the whites. They are seen as generous, well-behaved, and principled. While the white ladies of the missionary society talk about Christianity but don't put it into practice, the African-American congregation of the First Purchase Church put money in a collection for Helen Robinson. Although they are poor, they send gifts of food to Atticus as a sign of their gratitude after the trial. During the trial itself their response is restricted to an "angry muffled groan," and after Tom's death they are described as no more than "sulky" and "dissatisfied."

The African-American community's environment is also presented positively. Their houses are neat and snug with a warm and welcoming atmosphere, in sharp contrast to the unpleasant Ewell cabin in the same area. Their church is a poor building but is decorated with pride, and their cemetery is well looked after; Scout calls it "happy." Their spiritual leader, Reverend Sykes, shows a sensitivity and humanity lacking in many of the white characters. He insists on getting enough money for Helen Robinson and during the trial is concerned for the children's well-being.

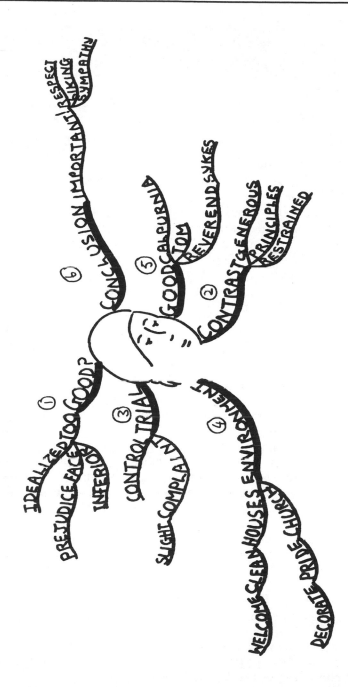

The two main African-American characters, Tom and Calpurnia, are also shown to be decent and virtuous. Tom is kind and compassionate. He is courteous and helpful to Mayella, and his whole bearing in court displays dignity and restraint. He doesn't accuse Mayella of lying, but says only that she must be mistaken. He is a family man, good to his wife and children, and his employer, Link Deas, exclaims in court that Tom is a good and reliable worker. Calpurnia is seen to be an excellent care-giver for the children, being firm with them when necessary, but always fair. The fact that Atticus trusts her and relies on her so much is a measure of Cal's excellence.

I do find the portrayal of the African-American community a little idealized and unrealistic. The only one who is at all unpleasant is Lula, who objects to the children's visit to the church. Her objection is rapidly stifled by the welcome the others extend to Cal's guests. However, the facts that emerge about the position of African-Americans speak for themselves. It becomes clear that their status is low. They are regarded as inferior by the whites. They are deprived of a good education – there are no African-American children at Scout's school – and so are nearly all illiterate. They can only work as servants or laborers. They are denied justice; Tom Robinson has no chance of a fair trial because the word of a black man will never be believed over the word of a white man. The book powerfully illustrates the position of black people in the South in the 1930s.

Harper Lee's attack on racial prejudice runs throughout the book. Part of her technique is to lead us to respect the African-American community. If she has exaggerated their goodness, it could be because she needs as much evidence as possible to fight the prejudiced, ignorant view that black people are inferior, a fight she presents movingly and convincingly.

GLOSSARY OF LITERARY TERMS

allegory a story that has a literal meaning and a symbolic meaning.

context the social and historical influences on the author; for example, the position of black people in America in the 1930s.

fable a story with a specific moral or message, usually made up by one person (as in *Aesop's Fables*).

image a kind of word picture used to make an idea come alive; for example, *it'd be sort of like shooting a mockingbird.*

irony **(dramatic)** where at least one character is unaware of an important fact that the reader knows about, and that is hinted at; **(simple)** ridiculing an opinion or belief by pretending to hold it, or pretending to be ignorant of the true facts.

metaphor a description of a thing as if it were something essentially different but also in some way similar; for example, *the starched walls of a pink cotton penitentiary.*

myth an ancient traditional story of gods and heroes, that has evolved over time and embodies popular ideas and beliefs.

personification a description of something abstract as if it were a person; e.g. *the remains of a picket drunkenly guarded the front yard.*

simile a comparison of two things that are different in most ways but similar in one important way; for example, *wriggling like a bucket full of catawba worms.*

theme an idea explored by an author; for example, prejudice

setting the place in which the action occurs, which usually affects the atmosphere; for example, Maycomb, the Radley house.

structure how the plot is organized; for example, in two parts, Part 1 focusing mainly on the children growing up and their dealings with Boo Radley, Part 2 with the trial and its aftermath.

viewpoint how the story is told; for example, through Scout's eyes, looking back at events that happened when she was a child.

INDEX